VOL .1

Beautiful Healing

Seven Love Letters for the Truth Seeker's Soul

Lee Felicia Dilbert

Printed in the United States of America
Email address: felicia@beautifulhealing.life
Website: www.beautifulhealing.life

ISBN: 978-1-7352848-2-8

Disclaimer: This book is the author's personal, non-fictional story. Every account in the book is true, and the events are portrayed to the best of the author's memory. While all the stories in this book are true, names and identifying details were eliminated to protect the privacy of the people involved. This book is not intended to be a substitute for the medical advice of a licensed physician or health professional. The reader should consult with their doctor or other health professional in any matters relating to his/her health. The author does not assume and hereby disclaims any liability to any party for any loss, damage, emotional distress, or disruption as a result of the book content.

Scriptures are taken from the Holy Bible, New International Version, NIV, Copyright 1973, 1978, 2011 by Biblica, Inc. All rights reserved worldwide. The "NIV" and "New International Version" are trademarks registered in the United States Patent and Trademark Office by Biblica, Inc.
Scripture marked NKJV are from the New Kings James Version, Copyright 1982 by Thomas Nelson. All rights reserved.
Scriptures marked NLT are from the Holy Bible, New Living Translation. 1996, 2004, 2007, 2013, 2015 by Tyndale House Foundation. Tyndale House Publishers, Carol Stream, Illinois 60188. All rights reserved.
Any internet addresses, books, products, blogs are offered as a resource and not intended in any way to imply an endorsement by BFF Publishing House.

BFF Publishing House is a Limited Liability Corporation dedicated wholly to the appreciation and publication of books for children and adults for the advancement of diversification in literature.

For more information on publishing contact:

Antionette Mutcherson at
bff@bffpublishinghouse.com
Website: bffpublishinghouse.com
Published in the United States by
BFF Publishing House
Atlanta, Georgia First Edition, 2020

Prologue

This book was completed in the year of global agony. 2020 will be remembered as the year of the COVID-19 pandemic and the soul-breaking reveal of the depths of systemic racism in America.

I will also remember 2020 as the year I finished a glorious assignment that the good Lord entrusted me with. He shared bits and pieces through dreams, confirmations, and miracles over the span of twenty years of my life. In 2016, shortly after my Mama was diagnosed with stage 4 lung cancer, the Lord woke me up early in the mornings and sent me more pieces through heavenly downloads. Now the puzzle is complete. You are holding all of them together in your hands.

Thank you, Jesus, for choosing me. I wrote exactly what you told me to. I'm willing to do whatever else you tell me to do, too. Lord, I love You, forever.

If there ever was a time to release Beautiful Healing, Volume 1, Seven Love Letters for the Truth's Seeker's Soul, it is now.

May this timeless message minister to your spirit for the rest of your days.

Lee and Phyllis Williams

Mama, you are forever my #1 girl. I shine bright because of all the light you loved inside of me. I miss you. I love you, forever.

Pop, you have a brilliant mind and a tender heart. I'm honored to call you my father. I love you, forever.

Dedication

This book is dedicated to my husband, Louis Lawrence Dilbert. I love you always and in all ways.

Acknowledgments

To My Publisher, Antionette Mutcherson, MBA:
Toni, these books are finally finished. Thank you for your dynamic professionalism, grace, patience, transparency, and heart. You ever so gently delivered my books. You are the smoothest book doula ever. The best is yet to come! I love you!

To Managing Editor, Riel Felice:
Sis! You get me. Thank you for every keystroke, every edit, every impromptu phone call, every laugh, every text and ever tear. You are one of a kind, Riel. I love you!

To My Dynamic Team:
Abigail Rew
Meleah Wallace
Lucia Riffel
Amoi Blocker

Sisters, I am SO honored to work with each of you. Your talents bring all my visions to life. I KNOW the good Lord hand picked each of you to serve Beautiful Healing!

To Michelle Gomez:
Thank you for your brilliance, kindness, and heart.

To LaShae Roberts:
I will forever appreciate you for showing me what unapologetic self-respect and worth looks like.

Dr. Kawana Johnson:
You are such a blessing! I thank God for you daily. The best is yet to come!

The Williams Family, 2020, Cynecia Manning/necieDIMPLE

To Lee Williams II:
My brotha! Thank you for the in-depth conversations, advice+ tips on the art of writing. You are appreciated. I love you, forever.

To Lee Alisha Williams:
Sis, thanks for your support and perspective!

To Lee Williams III:
Thank you for your encouragement. I love you, Moo Moo.

To my Angel:
Thank you so much.

To Lee Henry Williams (Pop):
Daddy, thank you for taking me to a Anthony Robbins "Awaken the Giant Within" conference in Atlanta, Ga. (1997). Thank you and I love you!

To everyone that has supported this effort with your time, talent, or treasure: I appreciate you. Thank you for believing in *Beautiful Healing, Vol. 1, 7 Love Letters for the Truth Seeker's Soul.* May the good Lord add abundant blessings to each of your lives.

This book was written for every woman who has lost her way.
Sister, your love letters have arrived.

With Love,

Felicia

Contents

Prologue 5

Dedication 7

Acknowledgments 9

Foreword 15

Introduction 17

A Love Letter to God 21

Love Letter 1: Unraveling 26

Love Letter 2: Releasing 48

Love Letter 3: Love 66

Love Letter 4: Truth 82

Love Letter 5: Peace 98

Love Letter 6: Worth 112

Love Letter 7: Embrace Your Path 128

"Peace I leave with you; my peace I give you. I do not give to you as the world gives. Do not let your hearts be troubled and do not be afraid." — John 14:27 (NIV).

The Lord has an interesting way of bringing us to a healing place. That place possesses divine peace, which surpasses all understanding. That place is one where our hearts are free to do what God has called us to do, where He has called us to do it, when we were appointed to. I imagine that for many people, that place of rest feels impossible to find. Depression, anxiety, guilt, shame, fear, worry, and regret are just a few emotions that can stifle a person's growth. These thieves of joy can leave one feeling tossed, turned, and, quite frankly, hopeless. But God.

We are all assigned gifts when we arrive on this Earth. Some people cultivate their gifts during their childhoods, while others discover theirs as adults. Either way, we all have a divine direction. The time has arrived to hope. To believe. To rest upon God's promises.

Imagine yourself walking alongside Felicia as she follows the voice of God in each letter within this book. I witnessed her patiently seeking the Lord with every word she wrote. Felicia has the most beautiful relationship and hears from our Lord and Savior, Jesus Christ daily. She is a warrior and guiding light who is now fully aware of her God and the gifts He has given her. Felicia's transparency continually impacts lives. Every day, my wife navigates her way through grief and trauma unlike any other person I know. I cherish the honor of witnessing her Beautiful Healing. Lee Felicia Dilbert is my joy.

May you be encouraged to believe that you, too, are an overcomer and that you can discover your path of Beautiful Healing. By the way, I'm also healing. Healing occurs over life and not overnight. View this book as a gift. May you experience Felicia's heart and desire to equip women with the tools to navigate life's challenges. To know their worth. May you rejoice in advance for the transformation you will experience, too. Go forth now and embrace your path of Beautiful Healing!

—Louis Lawrence Dilbert,
Husband

Introduction

This book is for every girl who yearned to be invited to the party and included in the circle. The girl who wished she had someone to talk to; someone with a positive listening ear; someone kind, loving, and real. Not quite an aunt; not quite a cousin. Someone like… a sister.

Well, sis, sit back and take a deep breath. Get super comfy. Prepare to read seven letters written just for you. For nearly three years, the Lord used my mind, heart, and hands to cultivate the content that now makes up this book. Get ready, love. I've got a feeling you are going to love this!

I want you to think back to a time when you were relatively young—let's say, between the ages of eight and ten. Can you remember what your personality was like? How did you see the world? What did you think when you noticed your face in the mirror? Did you smile? Well, my sister, there's one thing for sure: I know you were, and still are, beautiful. As the days went by and you grew older, did you experience changes that affected how you viewed yourself? My love, this book will mean many different things to you in many different ways. However, my prayer is that YOU receive the unshakable truth that YOU are valuable. That YOUR soul is beautiful. That YOU are loved. As I use my voice to tell my story, allow me to serve as an example of what it looks like to believe in yourself. I didn't get here overnight. Healing occurs over life.

If you have experienced abuse, manipulation, or any other heartbreaking situation, please allow these words to serve as the sincerest apology you never received. I, too, have been hurt. Deeply. I also once remained quiet when I knew the answer was to speak up. Intimidation and fear have a way of silencing women. You know what, though? I still managed to write this book. I didn't do it on my own, though. Sis, as you turn the pages, I pray that you fall in love with the custom-made message that the good Lord curated just for YOU to receive.

Let me ask you something. Do you agree that we, women, have a lot in common? Regardless of our skin color, hair texture, hobbies, choices, or financial realities, we are more alike than different. Can I get an amen? We all have aspirations and experiences;

we all desire to be loved. Every single one of us is valuable and deserves to be respected. Does every woman know this?

So, what's your current reality? Are you in a season of joy or pain? Perhaps, you are the picture of success to your friends; however, deep inside, you feel that something is just missing. Maybe you aren't 100% sure of your unique purpose. Or, perhaps, you are a loving mother, yet you feel invisible to the ones who matter most. Does fibromyalgia have you down? Are you carrying specks of bitterness from childhood? Do you yearn to show up for yourself in your life, but don't exactly know how? My love, may these words greet you warmly and ignite a fresh hope within you.

We may not have officially met just yet. However, it's safe to say that we both are trying to figure out how to navigate life. Well, I have good news! Girl, we don't have to think too hard. In the Bible, Psalm 119:105 states, "Your word is a lamp to my feet and a light to my path." That means that the directions are available, sis. Help is here! Let me tell you about a friend who changed my life. Growing up in South Georgia, I heard a lot about Him. My grandma's both talked to Him a lot. I was afraid at first because I didn't understand. One day, I learned more about His word and why I couldn't see Him. I was still confused. As I matured, everything became much clearer to me. I learned that Jesus was my Heavenly Father and that He created me for a distinct purpose. I found out that I was an original and despite all the unforeseen twists and turns I had experienced in life, there would be a great purpose for each one of them. One day, I understood that the Lord's infinite sovereign wisdom was right all along. Throughout this book, I share my love for my Heavenly Father and His word. I'm looking forward to hearing about how His love impacts your heart.

From my heart to your hands, I present to you, Beautiful Healing, Volume 1: Seven Love Letters for the Truth Seeker's Soul.

Prayer

Sister, I pray that each letter delivers rich nutrients to your mind, body, and spirit; that you embrace the Lord's ability to heal everything concerning you. While surrounded by love, I pray that you experience peace.
Most of all, I pray that you can see that you have a path in life—a real purpose.

Amen.

A Love Letter to God

Dear God,
As I sit in front of this mirror
looking deeply into my eyes,
I cannot deny what I see:
weariness,
pain,
sadness,
shame.
These burdens I cannot tote.
Today, I choose to lay down my ways.
Lord, I've been calling myself Your child;
however, I don't remember the last time I came to talk to You affectionately.

Can You forgive me for not saying hello regularly?
Can I surrender my heart to You right now, Lord?
I'm ready.
I'm finally ready to fully submit
with everything within me.
I'm willing to surrender—
RELEASE.
I'm making space to receive all of You now.
Your glory, Father, please come in.
My prayer is that my full heart will be graced by Your Holy Spirit.
At this moment, empower me to let go of the shattered pieces
from heartbreaks.
Heal heartaches.
Guide me to give up lifeless, bitter seeds.
I'm tired of this whirlwind.
As these tears slide down my heart, I rejoice.
I embrace this evidence that I am no longer numb.
Lord, unravel me beautifully;
I wanna feel Your presence.
Thank You, Father, for aligning my heart's work

with Your glory.
Grant me a freedom I have never known.
Lord, grant me a freedom I have never known.
Father, grant me a freedom I have never known.
I will not deny You this time.

She said He is your present help and she was right.
-Mama, Phyllis Marie Williams
-She said A charge to keep, I have and a God to glorify.
She was right.
Grandma, Ossie Bell Williams
You are never alone, Felicia;
the Lord is always with you.
-She was right.
My Nana, Margaret Acree

Lord, Jesus, You filled them with Your ways, love, and guidance—
Can you fill me up, too?
As I draw near to You, I hear You come closer to me.
It's a promise from Your word, right?
Okay, I'm scooting towards You, Lord.
Do you have a moment to come closer to me?

This sudden shift—
what is this new feeling?
Joy, indescribable!
Father, oh, precious Heavenly Father,
as the widest smile blooms from my face,
I recognize this fresh embrace.
Your grace has shown me my way;
Your mercy has led the way.
My goodness!
Your holy light illuminates Your will for my life;
I see my path of Beautiful Healing.
Now, I'm ready to walk in obedience, Heavenly Father.
Yes. Now, I'm ready.

The Path

Have you ever been lost before? The first time I visited Lenox Mall in Atlanta, I was so fascinated by the jazzy vibe, huge stores, and fashion that I forgot where I parked my car. This mall was a whole lot bigger than the Albany Mall, so I was truly lost. Where did I park? I thought. That's when I realized there was a huge mall map to my left. Getting lost in a mall is a piece of cake compared to getting lost in life. I have never met a woman who started her day saying, "You know what? I want to completely lose my way in life today." Who likes being lost? I would assume that no one does. I thought I knew where I was going with my life for a long while, only to realize that I had no idea. Several years passed before I stumbled upon my path. Sis, have you arrived at yours?

Imagine a path created just for you that was tailor-made by the Lord Almighty, specifically designed with your feet in mind, leading in a direction that only you can walk and arriving at a purpose that only you can fulfill. There are seemingly infinite possible paths in life, each unique and purposeful in their own way. So, then, how does a woman find her true path and trailblaze it? The first step is acknowledging that she is lost. Then, she must take time to reflect—to listen. I also believe that when she seeks the will that God has for her life, He will lead her. There is a distinct difference between a woman who is simply "doing life" by mechanically putting one foot in front of the other, versus a praying woman who is committed to embodying the character of Christ as she walks through life. The path of Beautiful Healing is the next step for the woman who is willing to ask, "How would Christ behave?" as she navigates her days. Her main priority is seeking him at the fork in her road. She's willing to exhibit his behavior every step of the way. Yes, that sister is walking the path of Beautiful Healing with a posture of obedience.

In 2016, I learned that once an individual survives their darkest night, they can then do one of two things: advance forward or remain stagnant. In the past, I figured that I would somehow find my way through life. Hope kept me trudging along through uncertainty, but then, I embraced the truth: the Lord directs my path and guides me forward. I acknowledged that hope simply would not be enough. While reflecting, I found that I had to free myself in order to arrive at my tailor-made destination. I hope you see yourself in my story. We all have a purpose. Your path awaits.

Reflection Time

You will find reflection questions after each letter. Use these questions to learn more about yourself. Now, don't overthink. Do what feels good to you, sis.

Love Letter 1
Unraveling

Dear Sis,

Beauty. How do you define it? According to Webster's Dictionary, beauty is defined as "a particularly graceful, ornamental, or excellent quality." The moment a woman encounters beauty, she shall never forget it.

First, it was her touch. Then, her smile. My first encounter with beauty was with my mother, Phyllis Marie Williams. My first memory is of her singing "Happy Birthday" to me with a big smile on her face. It was my fifth birthday. When I looked into her bluish-grey eyes, I always saw compassion. Her laugh was literally the sound of joy. To know her was to love her. As a little girl, I had no clue that such a marvelous soul was nestled within all those warm hugs. I fondly remember the Saturdays before Easter when she helped me with my Easter speeches. Even though I kept forgetting the words, Mama would patiently say, "Okay, try one more time, Felicia."

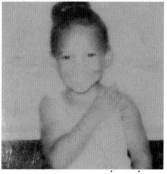

As a preteen, I couldn't have fathomed how deep Mama's anointed love for Jesus was. That same anointing is what eventually led me to my path of Beautiful Healing. The Lord knew the connection I would have with my mother. We shared a loyal friendship filled with prayer, a lot of belly laughs, and the frequent miracle. I learned from her every day through observation. The curriculum was the Holy Bible and the teacher was Jesus. Mama often reminded me that she was only the vessel. She always gave the Lord glory. For the sunshine.

For her family. For everything. The Lord ordained her to be my Mama and to educate me. Her ways became mine. As I write this, I realize once again what an absolute gift she was. Being ushered into womanhood surrounded by her unconditional motherly love continues to be EVERYTHING for me and my siblings. Mama enjoyed being a mama. One day, I looked back over all the years and realized the source of her gentleness, loving-kindness, and grace. I clearly saw that Mama ultimately held my hand and led me straight to my Heavenly Father, Jesus Christ, one "I love you" at a time.

The Unknown

I knew something was wrong when I didn't receive a call on August 1, 2016. You see, Mama and I always sang "Happy Birthday" to each other every year. It was one of our timeless traditions. Well, that year, I celebrated with my husband, Louis, and friends at my favorite Thai restaurant in Atlanta. I kept checking my phone to see if I happened to miss Mama's call. Even though I was in my late thirties, I still longed to hear her voice on my birthday. I could feel that something just wasn't quite right. I quietly stepped away from the table and dialed her number. After three rings, she answered.

"Hey, Esha! Girl, I was gon' call you. Happy birthday, baby."
Even though she was saying happy words, she sounded so far away. And weak.

"Thank you, Mama. What have you been up to? You feeling okay?" I asked.

"Well, my back is hurting a little bit. I'm about to go lay down for the night."

It was 6:30 in the evening. Mighty early to be laying down for the night, I thought. I wondered why she was going to bed so early but didn't want to pry.

"Esha, I will talk to you later, baby. Tell Louis hello for me. Y'all drive safe, okay?"

"Yes, ma'am. Love you, Mama," I replied.

No birthday song. My gut was telling me that something was wrong, and it was right. That was the beginning of the end of Mama as I had always known her.

When I got home from Atlanta, I went to visit her. When I entered the house, I immediately discerned trouble. Something was very wrong; I could feel it in my stomach. When I saw her face, I instantly knew that she wasn't feeling good. She tried to deflect my attention by talking about the weather. I couldn't have cared less about the fall breeze, though. Why was her laughter so faint? My concern heightened when Mama kept glancing away instead of looking at me.

After several awkward moments, she nervously suggested that we walk outside to get some fresh air.

As we approached the front door, she grabbed my hand. Hers felt so fragile in mine. Everything about this visit was offbeat. I opened the door and the breeze embraced us as we walked out. She and I shared silence and gazed at the evening sky, splashed, and tinted with gentle shades of lavender and tangerine. Then, she told me. "Esha, you know I've been smoking them cigarettes for a long time."

Our eyes met for the first time that day. I saw the sadness in her bluish-grey eyes. "Oh, Mama," was all I could say. I held her hand a little tighter. Then, I gently pulled her closer to me and kissed her on the forehead, just like she had always kissed me during my pain. The tears began to fall. We both wiped each other's tears away. We felt each other's pain, just like always. Then, she leaned over and whispered, "Baby, I ain't got long."

The tangerine Tallahassee sky no longer had any lavender; the sun would set soon. My stomach began to ache. Even though my chest felt tight, I managed to hold Mama in my arms as she rested her head on my heart. I mustered up a weak, "Aww, Suga, now, we gon' get through this." Mama used to repeat these same words to me during my darkest depressive episodes. No matter how low I was, these eight words always lifted my spirits. Surely, I could count on these eight words in that sad moment, standing on the porch with Mama. After all, now was my chance to save her day, just as she always had saved mine.

The words didn't sound right, though. Instead of sounding upbeat and strong, my voice cracked. The heartbreak had stolen all of my strength. No Superwoman approach could withstand cancer. Mama smiled at me because she knew what those words meant. She knew I was trying. Then, she kissed me on the cheek. Instinctively, we hugged each other tighter. The tears continued to fall.

The time on the porch felt odd, yet peaceful. The silence was loud. Her voice was dampened by this bad news, yet I saw peace in her eyes as she told me the truth. She always was a truth-teller. All of my tears were serving a deeper supernatural purpose within me. They loosened the proverbial mask that I had hidden behind for Lord knows how long. The mask with the permanent smile—you know, the one that's supposed to cover up how you really feel inside. The one that protects you from getting hurt. The one that blocks authenticity. That mask. I had come undone and Mama could tell.

"I know you're scared, baby," she told me. "I am, too. You know what, though, Esha? You can survive without me, baby. You are really, really strong, baby. Like, stronger than you ever could know."

Our tears fell harder. My body shook and my soul ached. The final remnants of that metaphorical mask loosened. Eventually, I imagined it falling to the ground and shattering. While still holding hands and with red, puffy eyes, we watched the rays of the dwindling sunset in the evening sky, both of us raw and heartbroken. In due time, I would realize the power of that moment on the porch that October evening. Mama's sunset would usher me into a new supernatural and unbreakable connection with Jesus Christ.

My Broken Peace

I was never told how I was supposed to handle hard times in life. I didn't recall that being in the daily routine of everyday life. No hints were on TV, either. As circumstances would have it, sis, we both began to experience the darkest season of our lives: my Mama was diagnosed with Stage 4 Small Cell Lung Cancer. Oh, my God. The reality of her looming death shook me to the core. I simply did not know how to process this news.

The days to come would bring scary situations and sadness. The future held repeat visits to the cancer treatment center, multiple trips to the pharmacy, and lots of questions. I still can't imagine how she must have felt going through all of this. I witnessed her experience awful nausea, aches, and full body pain. My body shared Mama's pain. I began to have an agitating gnawing in my belly. Our hair thinned. She was nauseous just about every single day. We both wrestled with anticipatory grief, a type of grief that occurs before an impending loss. We were so scared.

I felt lower and lower every day as each part of my heart broke. The strong, inconsiderate winds of grief blew harder each day as my family continued to receive bad news. My faith was shaken. I was always told that Jesus would be a present help in times of need, but I couldn't help but think, Where is God?!

I felt the heaviness. Per usual, depression had shown up unannounced. Unfortunately, this was not our first time meeting;

this illness entered my life when I was a young child.

Unclear

I was in denial about how bad my headaches were and figured that my vomiting was induced by grief. I made excuses about taking a deeper look at my symptoms. I thought things like, This must just be a sinus headache. Mom is on her deathbed, so what business do I have complaining about a minor headache? Even though I hadn't felt well for several months, I kept pushing forward as best as I could—after all, isn't this the picture of strength? I was the oldest of all my parent's children. What kind of example am I setting? I thought to myself one morning as I struggled to get out of the bed. I just didn't have the strength. I hated myself because I felt like I was failing Mama.

On February 2, 2017, I saw my primary care doctor for my annual check-up. I shared all the symptoms I was experiencing with him. He suggested that I go have blood work done. A week later, I was informed that my results came back just fine. My doctor couldn't find anything wrong. I shrugged my shoulders and left. The following week, my symptoms got worse. I returned to the doctor's office for a second opinion. Again, he found nothing. During that visit, he suggested that I see a local endocrinologist. He sent the endocrinologist's office my referral, and when the nurse called me a few days later, she stated that they had no available appointments until May 2. That was three months later. What was I supposed to do in the meantime? Three months seemed like forever. I made the appointment anyway and figured I would continue to push on despite my intermittent symptoms. May 2 would just be another day, I thought to myself. As I hung up the phone, I felt another wave of nausea. I wanted to go see Mama later that day. I prayed that I would be able to make it. I felt guilty for feeling so out of it. Pull it together, girl, I would tell myself. I still felt physically sick, though.

Mom's health declined rapidly in March of 2017. In her last days, I couldn't think clearly and began to have the worst headaches of my life. Despite illness, we still shared timeless, precious moments. She prayed for me and I prayed for her. We laughed so hard one day that the stubborn partition of cancer completely lifted! For a few moments, we were just two chicks laughing out loud with no barriers. The bond of love we shared is indescribably pure; so very beautiful. Oh, what a gift from God that moment was. Ah, those truly unforgettable moments of unconditional, agape love. Thank you for those, Jesus.

Louis, my sweet husband, always had a way of making Mama laugh. Thanks to Louis, my family got a chance to hear that endearing, distinct, and hearty laugh a few more times before Mama left us. Towards the end, Mama's personality became more and more childlike. One evening, Louis surprised her with a game of peek-a-boo while she laid in the hospital bed in my parents' room. She was in good spirits that day. She laughed so loud! Louis had her so tickled! She was so carefree, like a little girl. I knew Mama didn't have much time left with us. The glimpses of childlikeness were indicators that she was returning to the state in which she entered the world—a baby. By the grace of God, I was completely present and able to embrace these moments.

I woke up the next morning and knew I needed to go see her immediately. I knew I had to move quickly. When I walked into the bedroom, I could see that she would not be with us much longer. She was completely quiet for most of my visit. I read the 23rd Psalm to her, then began to gather my things and was about to head out when Mama stopped me.

"Esha, thank you for coming to see me. You the best. I will always love you, baby," she told me. I was stunned. Oh, Mama, I love you, too," I said. I walked back to the bed, kissed her, and talked to her some more. However, she said nothing else to me. I had received my last words.

My mother went home to be with Jesus on April 25, 2017. I'll admit, I felt a ton of different emotions, including peace that she was with the Lord; anger that she would never meet my children; sadness that my sister would never get to share her college experiences with Mama and that Mama wouldn't get to see my nephew, Benjamin, grow up; heartache that she wouldn't see my youngest brother graduate from FAMU ten days after she died; and sadness that she wouldn't grow older with Daddy. I knew she was no longer in pain and suffering. Even still, our family was in so much agony.

So, May 2 came. It was time for me to go to the doctor. However, May 2 didn't turn out to just be another day. It was now the day before Mama's funeral. As much as I wanted to cancel the doctor's appointment, I knew Mama would want me to go. I could think of a million reasons why I didn't want to go, and they were all valid. However, Mama would have pushed me to go take care of myself if she was still alive and I knew it. That morning, I felt like I had been hit by a truck. I had the worst headache, my vision was strained, and I even had trouble standing up. I could hardly make it out of the door.

I arrived and managed to check in. Not long afterward, a beautiful and very compassionate registered nurse delicately told me that she had reviewed my blood work results from February of 2017. From what she could see, it was clear that I had Type 2 Diabetes.

"Your A1C is so high that you could have easily gone into a coma."

I was stunned. Was she looking at the wrong paperwork and test results? Surely, my primary doctor had not missed that I was diabetic in February.

"How have you been feeling, Felicia?" she asked.

"Awful, Miss," I mustered.

"Have you had any or all of the following symptoms: fatigue, weight gain, nausea, low cognitive functioning, headaches, forgetfulness, or mood swings?"

"Yes, I have dealt with all of those, ma'am."
All the while, I linked all my symptoms to anticipatory grief. Every time I vomited, struggled to get out of bed, or felt confused, I just figured I was overwhelmed with grief.

"Miss, my mother's funeral is tomorrow. I don't know what to make of all of this. I hear what you are saying, but are you 100% sure that I really have Type 2 Diabetes?"

"Yes, Felicia. You do," the nurse stated. "I am so sorry that your doctor didn't treat you for this condition in February."

I remained in the medical office for what felt like three hours.

"Felicia, I cannot tell you not to go to your mother's funeral. I have also lost my mother. It is an awful feeling to lose a mom," the kind nurse expressed to me. I appreciated how she validated my feelings by acknowledging them. I even saw tears in her eyes. What an angel, right? It was not by accident that this particular nurse was tending to me. Nope. Even on one of the hardest days of my life, the Lord was still mindful of me.

"Felicia, I don't want to alarm you, but you are very sick.

Please remember to take care of yourself during these circumstances. Please."

Still in complete shock, I gathered my items. Weary and spent, I somehow managed to walk to my car. I faintly remember her saying something about following up with my primary physician. I'll never forget how long the walk back to my car felt. I remember clenching my steering wheel and wondering, "Will my family be burying me next?"

The next morning, I could feel the tension in my back as I opened my eyes. Sitting up, I noticed a piercing headache and wave of nausea taking over. Pain enveloped me. Every cell in my body knew that today hurt. It's interesting how bodies hold trauma.

Everything in me was heartbroken. My Louis held my hand throughout the entire drive to Georgia. As we entered the front door of the church in Pelham, Georgia, I felt a strong presence of peace. My husband continued to hold my hand firmly as we joined my siblings and father on the front row. There Mama was, dressed in the really pretty purple dress with the pop of silver on the neckline—the dress that she fell in love with in the nice store in Tampa. As I looked at her, I managed to smile. Mama was finally at peace. No more cancer, just resting. I took a deep breath, embracing the honor of being her oldest child. While getting dressed earlier that morning, I decided that I would not share my condolences at the funeral. I just didn't think I could handle it. I often had panic attacks over lesser matters, and the news from the day before still lingered.

Surely, I figured I wouldn't have the strength to give Mama proper respects. However, when the preacher asked if any immediate family members would like to share any final remarks, I found myself standing. Louis escorted me as I gracefully approached the podium. Holding the microphone, my eyes locked with my Louis and I could feel my strength rising. I began opening my heart to the congregation: "My Mama was a true lady. Loved the Lord, loved her family, and loved me, despite my struggles." All in all, I saluted my mother's legacy dynamically. I didn't struggle to remember any particular words to share; my heart did all the talking. Only God can deposit a strength like that. Goodness, mercy, peace, and love led me through the rest of the day. The Lord came to my rescue by armoring me to do the very thing I never thought I could. I can do all things through Christ, who strengthens me (Philippians 4:13).

The following week, I felt faint and was hospitalized due to complications of Type 2 Diabetes. Nothing is ever under control, I thought to myself while lying in the hospital bed. Sadly, the hospital had become such a familiar territory. Even though my Louis was right there, I felt alone—so alone. How was I going to get through this? Suddenly, the memory of that cool October night in 2016 came to mind. That night, Mama told me how strong I was and that I could live without her. As the tears fell down my face, I tried to imagine how so. It seemed impossible. I closed my eyes and prayed. That was my only choice. Sis, have you ever felt utterly helpless?

After I was released from the hospital, I fearfully visited my primary physician. He apologized profusely for his oversight regarding my blood work. He explained the dangerous connection between diabetes and heart disease. I learned that heart disease starts with high blood sugar levels, which can damage arteries. The arteries become stiff and hard over time, thus increasing the chances of a heart attack or stroke. Now educated on my condition, I left the office slightly encouraged to face this situation, but also really shell-shocked. Was I going to be alright?

I decided to stop by the park that overlooked the water before I went home. Water usually calmed me down. My phone rang. It was my husband. I answered the phone with tears in my eyes.

"Hello...? Hey, dear... I can't do this, Lou. I'm so scared!"

"Baby, baby, slow down, okay? Breathe. That's my girl. Okay, what did the doctor say?" He responded.

"He told me I gotta make some changes—quick!" I panicked.

"Well, if you have to change your eating habits, then so do I. I've got your back, babe. You ain't going to go at this alone. We will fight this together!" He encouraged me.

I took a deep breath, recognizing the hope within my husband's words. Even though I felt scared, I didn't have to give up. I could experience a better life. I still had a chance at one filled with health and harmony. That was the moment when I committed to changing the unhealthy habits that led to the diagnosis. I would stop eating mindlessly, making excuses about taking my medications, and being so hard on myself. I imagined myself conquering this condition by adopting the heart-healthy meal plan my doctor suggested. I envisioned myself exercising several times a week. I felt empowered.

Louis and Felicia Dilbert, Dorothy B. Oven Park

Unavailable

Although I felt hopeful the day prior, my motivation proved to be inconsistent. The loud reality that Mama was really gone echoed in my mind. I missed how she encouraged me on my hardest days. Memories rushed in. Before cancer, Sunday was the day the whole family gathered at around 6 p.m. to enjoy Mama's cooking, endless laughter, and pure joy. No matter who had an attitude with who, or what looming deadlines approached us on Monday, we could all count on Sunday afternoon to make it all better. If you peered into the kitchen, you would see this scene: lots of belly laughs, friendly jokes, and plenty of permissible interruptions in conversation. I filled the cups with ice, my brother put the plates on the table, my sister took care of the silverware, and mom could be heard saying, "Time to eat, y'all!" Love. Love. Love! Our souls collectively exhaled on Sunday evenings. Familiar faces resembling happy hearts deeply connected; oh, what a sight to behold! Our beautiful family at dinnertime.

Phyllis M. Williams (Mama), 2015
Mama just finished cooking one of her legendary Sunday dinner's

I vividly remember the after-dinner routine of cleaning off the table, helping mom with the dishes, and hesitantly saying my goodbyes. Mama always prepared a to-go plate for me. As I walked towards the door to leave, Mama would always call me one last time, "Esha! Wait, baby. Let me walk you out." That was her way, never missing an opportunity to pour a little more love in my heart. I would look over my shoulder, smiling, and say, "I love you, Mama! Thank you for dinner." For many months, memories like these caused me to grieve deeply. My motivation was crushed, which threatened my decision to pursue a healthier lifestyle.

Unfortunately, the pain was an unwelcome guest and was having its way in my marriage. Louis and I began to argue constantly. I felt that he wasn't qualified to give me advice because he hadn't suffered the same loss I had. Therefore, everything he said to me felt really fake. Our friendship took a hit. Times were tense. Louis was only trying to help, but my patience was raw. I pushed him away. No matter how much I tried, I couldn't shake the grief.

One day, I decided to sort through Mama's belongings. I thought it would ease my pain—wrong. I began to wear her old outfits and shoes. I told myself it was a way to celebrate her memory. Every garment felt so heavy, though. Looking back, I can clearly see how unprepared I was to sort through those clothes. It was too soon. I was unintentionally making matters worse. One day, Louis brought it to my attention.

"Baby, let me help you with this, okay? Can't you see how much this is hurting you? All of these clothes represent your pain. Let me help," he told me. I became angry with him. Looking back, I feel for my husband. I really gave him a hard time.

That next week, I tried to do my makeup, a hobby, and commonality that Mama and I shared; however, it didn't come out right. Everything that once brought me happiness now caused so much sadness. I was depressed. Everything was a mess. I weighed 270 pounds. Diabetes had wrecked my skin and ravaged my hair. On most days, I was emotional and exhausted. My new normal was pure hell.

After a routine check-up with my primary care doctor, I learned that the combination of stress, Type 2 Diabetes, and weight gain was putting me at greater risk for a heart attack. My Lord was all I could think. That evening, Louis sat me down and said, "Baby, we've gotta do something about all of this." He suggested that I rest and wholeheartedly pursue healing. With his blessing, I worked fewer hours, avoided overwhelming situations, and began to write—a favorite pastime of mine. He suggested that we go to therapy together. That was the first time I felt like Louis understood my pain. I was tired of pushing him away. I loved him! I was so angry, though; I missed my mom. The inner conflict was exhausting. I experienced a breakthrough when my husband looked me in my eyes and told me that he was moving in the valley with me: "You don't have to walk in the dark alone, baby. Scoot over. I'm moving in, too." I could see the love in his eyes. It made my heart feel warmer—no chill. This is why I will love my Louis forever and why I want to have his children. There is no other man like my Lou. I listened to him intently that night. Really listened. Phone off, TV off, ears open. I confessed how tired I was— tired of being "the strong one," tired of being a soft spot for hard people to land on, tired of depression, tired of being overweight. Our conversation was healing and cathartic. We hadn't connected like this in a long while.

I decided to finally get rid of the metaphorical Superwoman cape. It was too tight, anyway. Instead, I committed to:
- Spending time in reflection
- Writing
- Resting
- Getting my hips in bed at a decent hour
- Quit Worrying
- Quit People Pleasing

It was time to live again. I accepted that I couldn't solve everyone's problems and embraced that rest was a good thing. I realized that focusing on myself was perfectly okay. During this season of my life, I embodied an unapologetic perspective. With absolutely no strength to worry about what other people thought of me, I established healthy boundaries in every 'ship in my life, meaning that I stopped putting other people's feelings before my own. I was trying to live! Sacrificing my health for frivolous conversations, coffee dates, and window shopping? No, thanks—time-out! I established boundaries in my relationships with my acquaintances, friends, and family. All the 'ships had to remain at the dock. One night, a co-worker texted me asking if we could talk because she needed to vent.

I texted her, "No, sis. I'm going to pray for you, though." I sent her a voice memo of the prayer and let that be. I remember feeling very light after that. What was that? Peace. I had done enough. I didn't feel guilty at all, actually. The choice to have these direct conversations freed me. I said what I needed to say. When I studied Communications at Valdosta State University, I learned about the power of words. Sis, oftentimes we know exactly what we need to say to people. My desire to get healthy empowered me to speak my truth. Here are some examples of how I started communicating:

When I received an invitation to something that I did not want to attend, I responded, "I really appreciate the invitation; however, I cannot attend." No additional words needed to be said!

I ran into a friendly acquaintance at the nail salon and she asked me, "May I call you later this week to catch up? It was so nice seeing you." I knew that I was practicing more self-care by not engaging in deep conversations with others, but she didn't have to know all of that.

Therefore, I responded in a very friendly way, "Sis, it has been awesome catching up with you today! How about we exchange emails?" I did what was best for me.

My homegirl called me later that week. She said, "Felicia, I want to run something by you. I think my boyfriend is taking advantage of me. Sis, I know you will tell me the truth! Am I tripping, or what?" I responded, "Sis, how are you doing? It is good to hear from you. C'mon, now, think back on all of those conversations we had. What do you think about the situation? You've got this, girl. Much love. Let me catch you another time. Have a blessed night."

We all have people in our life who always have one more question, a thought they want to share, or something they just want to get off their chest. I have even been that person before! These are the people who text you repeatedly if you don't respond right away or call and leave a message, then text you to see if you got their voicemail. I love my needy folk; however, I taught them that I was serious by unapologetically (and sometimes temporarily) blocking them on my phone. That's right. That action spoke louder than words! No love lost, sis. I simply chose me over we.

Sis, you've got to stand your ground with people. Don't let anyone push you around. Don't stay at work late. Leave when it's quitting time. Jobs don't keep you warm at night. Respect yourself.

Folks can wait. Remember: with every reply sent and phone call answered, you are silently communicating that you don't really respect your boundaries. Others realize this, as well. Back up your words with actions.

These boundaries allowed me the breathing space necessary for my optimal healing. My prayer is that you allow yourself to experience the freedom and peace that you have always deserved. Only you can determine when enough is enough! This, my dear, is why boundaries are crucial for healing—because really and truly, we cannot save anyone but ourselves.

My new outlook on life consisted of focusing on losing weight, having more energy, and practicing mindfulness. I was committed to conquering Type 2 Diabetes. Having Louis's support was an added bonus.

The time came to purge the refrigerator and freezer. I felt overwhelmed about the money wasted and somewhat guilty for throwing away all the food, even though it was so unhealthy. When we got to the freezer, I thought I would cry. All that good ice cream was going in the trash! Dang. Thankfully, Louis lightened my mood by making jokes while we threw out the bad stuff. He always knew how to make me laugh.

Day by day, I kept the promise I made to myself and started making smarter choices to sustain my lifestyle change. When I embraced that my routine now consisted of needles, glucose tablets, and fluctuating blood sugar levels that I was now committed to regulating, the depression began to lift. I still felt yucky just about every day, but I kept going.

Louis and I attended nutritional classes, where we learned about blood sugar and how to correctly administer my medications. Louis's devotion to my wellness inspired me. His faith was contagious. His hope empowered my pursuit of healing on every level.

Diabetes management taught me how to remain content while also empowering myself. I decided that I would thrive despite this debilitating condition and that depression, grief, anxiety, and fear were not going to control me. Liberation! I wouldn't be denied anything in life due to this diagnosis. I learned that there would never come a day when it would be necessary to EVER hide my truth. I began to do something that my Grandma Ossie used to do: declare God's word and goodness over my life. Alas, I unapologetically managed my health and didn't allow fear to manage me.

Untangled

The process of illness is synonymous with the shedding of dead life. As healing superseded my frailty, a metamorphosis was ignited within me. I emerged completely free—there was no more mask to hide behind. Trudging forward after losing my mother taught me a new language, an understanding of how to express the unexpressed, a way to understand the universal pain of women. My emotional intelligence, discernment, and transparency increased tenfold. Transformation propelled me to seek deeper truth. I reckoned with the question, "Do I really know the Lord?" My spirit was not at peace with the answer. I confessed that I knew bits and pieces about religion, but not about fostering a pure relationship with God. I accepted Christ when I was 12. However, I didn't know the Lord for myself. At this point in my life, I had no other choice but to search for my identity in Christ. I yearned to learn who He really was. I started studying the Bible. I listened, learned, sought, then sought again. Louis and I joined a phenomenal church in Tallahassee, Florida. Sis, I wanted to be refreshed in a completely new way. My life literally depended on it. I yearned to apply God's word. I was even willing to unlearn the strong dependency I had on other people. Any validation that I needed, I wanted directly from the Lord.

Although I always had the best of intentions, I clearly saw that I always leaned on Mama's faith instead of developing my own. I didn't know the lover of my soul, Jesus. I knew how to pray; however, I didn't know how to dwell in prayer. You see, I always thought Mama would be there. I never accepted that I would have to spend even one day without her, let alone months or years.

Therapy helped me to see that my identity had been wrapped up in my mother and my love for her. I never imagined that our weekly kitchen chats would end. I had all my needs met and big laughs, with a great Mama to match. Why live my purpose, dig for greatness, or seek understanding? I always went to her and she worked it all out, so there was that. Of course, I prayed while my mother was alive, but I never had to wait long for those prayers to be answered. I was too busy asking Mama to solve all my problems or talking her head off. Why would I look up and seek the truth? Mama's faith always saved the day.

My breakthrough came when I realized that everything good that Mama had deposited into me came from my good, good Father in Heaven. That was a strong "aha" moment. If she drew closer to Him, so could I. One of my favorite Bible verses is Romans 8:28, "And we know that all things work together for the good of those that love God, to them who are called according to His purpose." I accepted the Lord at age 12—now, I wanted to get to know Him.

In order for everlasting change to occur, I needed to trust the word of God to unravel and rebuild my heart. Life as I once knew it had changed. I needed to grow. I stopped allowing negative beliefs, especially the subtle ones, to run my life. I couldn't be out here playing. I leaned on the Word like never before. I was ready to run after Him until I couldn't run anymore. The word of God teaches in 2 Corinthians 5:17, "I am a new creation. Old things have passed away and all things have been made new." I wrote this verse on an index card and repeatedly rehearsed it in my mind until I had committed it to memory.

Unapologetic

Daily, I walk in the light of my Mama's legacy, realizing that she was right about me. I, Felicia Dilbert, am stronger than I ever believed myself to be. I celebrate every step I take; movement is life. All glory goes to God. I'm grateful that my Louis constantly teaches me that I am worth growing for. Sis, you are worth growing for, too. Sis, please don't limit growth to only pursuing a job, obtaining a degree, or planning your dream vacation. You are worthy of growing for your OWN well-being. That's right. YOU are worthy, NOW!

With so much love,
Felicia

NOTE TO
SELF

1. _What are your thoughts about love letter 1?_

_____

_____

_____

_____

_____

_____

_____

_____

_____

_____

_____

_____

_____

2. _What breakthroughs/positive outcomes does a woman stand_

to experience as a result of a season of unraveling?

_____

_____

_____

_____

_____

_____

_____

_____

_____

_____

_____

3. _What does physical unraveling look like to you?_

Emotional? Relational?

_____

_____

_____

_____

_____

_____

_____

_____

_____

_____

_____

NOTE TO
SELF

4. What powerful lessons have you learned from difficult seasons in your life?

_____

_____

_____

_____

_____

_____

_____

_____

_____

_____

_____

_____

_____

5. *List any important take-aways from the 1st love letter.*

_____

_____

_____

_____

_____

_____

_____

_____

_____

_____

_____

_____

_____

_____

Love Letter 2
Releasing

Dear Sis,

One summer evening, I sat at my kitchen table and wrote: Purpose, where are you? Can you show yourself? Lord, show me why You created me. Let me hear from you, Heavenly Father. Okay, what direction should I go in? I need you to be really specific because you know I get lost easily, God. LOL! So, I need some strength for the days ahead. I want a new life. Just like animals have instincts and know how to survive, I, too, want to know where to go, how to go, and when to go, Jesus. Make it plain, please. Amen.

Have you ever felt like this, sis? C'mon, honey, let's go for a walk. Girl, I will tell you how the Lord led me through a season I refer to as "releasing."

While I cleaned off the kitchen table on another ordinary Sunday afternoon, I glanced at the Bible on the bookshelf. I decided to stop cleaning and open the Bible. The pages flipped open to the parable about the lame man, found in the fifth chapter of the book of John. There was a pool in Jerusalem where many disabled people gathered. They believed that every once in a while, when the water was stirred, the first to enter it would be healed. Among the crowd, there lay a man that had been there for 38 years. When Jesus saw the man lying there and learned that he had been in this condition for a long time, he asked him, "Do you want to get well?"

"Sir," the disabled man replied, "I have no one to help me into the pool."

"Get up! Pick up your mat and walk," Jesus said to him.

My path in life had become predictable. I was tired of being sick. I often felt sluggish. Over time, I watched others progress in life. I grew comfortable hiding in the shadows. I could be found laying down during life's milestones. Depression overtook me. Deep down inside, I still believed that maybe I was created with distinct skills and gifts from the Creator. There was a specific path created for a specific purpose, just for me, right? How could I find my special path, though? Despite my circumstances, I was willing to trust that there was hope for me and continually pray for the directions.

My first day working at the Florida State University Life Coaching Center was in June of 2017. When I entered the William Johnston Building, I entered a whole new world. I was intrigued by this role from the very beginning. Early on, I could feel that this role would serve a dynamic purpose in my life. It wasn't just any ol' job. Life coaching is specifically aligned with my heart for service and empowerment, as well as my God-given strengths. I met my new co-workers, participated in a tour of the building, and got settled into my new spacious office. I loved the environment instantly. Management encouraged all the newbies to decorate their offices in a way that reflects their own personal styles. Everything about this opportunity felt incredible.

The first two weeks were filled with training. Management covered all the details; therefore, there was no room for guesswork. I appreciated that. This was a place where caring about people was welcomed. I was in the right spot. My primary responsibility consisted of meeting with diverse students on a one-on-one basis each week. The students were all so different, yet the same in a lot of ways. I was glad to serve by referring students to resources on campus and being a listening ear. I quickly familiarized myself with all the resources on campus. It felt good to go to work on Monday mornings, and on Sunday evenings, I found myself looking forward to the beginning of a new week.

My career finally had a purpose. I had found my rhythm. Mama had been gone for about three months at this point. Sometimes, the grief felt like it was completely gone; other times, it trampled me out of nowhere. Some days, I would smile at all the good times. Other days, I felt more reflective, and slowly, between my smiles, the memories of her brought great sadness. Oh, how I missed my favorite girl. She was like a sister and a really good friend at the same time—my mama/sister/friend. Just that morning, I had written in my journal that I knew Mama would be so proud of me. If she was here, she would say something like, "Girl, I knew you was going to get that job! Get it, sis!" I smiled at first, only to feel down seconds later. Have you ever felt happy and sad at the same time?

One day after work, Anita Baker's "Giving You the Best That I Got" came on the radio. Memories of morning car rides to middle school came to mind. Mama loved her some Anita Baker! That particular song was her favorite. She would play that tape to no end! When I arrived home from work, I ignored my sadness by diverting attention to cleaning the counter, then preparing dinner. I buried myself in the busyness. No matter how much I tried to distract myself, I couldn't shake the sadness that night. I stayed up pretty late.

I woke up late the next morning. While rushing to get dressed, I texted my manager. Unfortunately, around lunchtime, I began to feel nauseous. I clearly wasn't having a good day. I struggled through my afternoon coaching sessions. By 5:00 p.m., I could feel my joy waning.

I gradually began to call into work late due to nausea. I was trying really hard not to fall off. I felt defeat rising up, though. Per usual, things just weren't turning out right. From the very beginning, I knew that this opportunity was different. So, I needed to stay on my feet. I had to. I did a lot of things in hopes of a quick turnaround—I changed my diet, joined a grief group, and tried a new medication for Type 2 Diabetes. I was giving it the best that I had.

My body wasn't having it. It rejected healing. Unfortunately, nausea, frequent restroom breaks, and headaches were now daily occurrences. Even though I had changed my diet and lost nearly 75 pounds, I was still struggling. I ran to the bathroom during my lunch break, all the while thinking about what would happen if I lost this job. What was I going to do? I laid up against the wall in the stall and prayed as I cried: Lord, now... I really love this job... You've got to heal me so that I can thrive for once! You made me to love people... and I'm loving them. I love my job. I think you still have a plan for me... A lot has been going wrong in my life for a long time... I need a win, God. I need a win. Jesus, give me strength. Come through for me, please.

While washing the mascara off my face, I recited the 23rd Psalm: "The Lord is my Shepherd, I shall not want..." Feeling hopeless, I headed back to my office while praying for more strength to make it through the rest of the day without vomiting. I committed to fighting as hard as I could to stay in the game, even though I didn't feel like I was going to make it.

I yearned to be free in order for my supervisors, coworkers, and students to really see me for me. I was tired of my greatness being overshadowed by illness. I was more than Diabetes! More than depression! More than anxiety! More than anything, I was exhausted from it all.

With fresh hope, I decided that I would not give up—no matter what. I found a Bible verse to recite every hour. I set my phone alarm to remind me. I tapped into a growth mindset. I extended more grace to myself. I was doing my absolute best, even though I wasn't succeeding in the way I envisioned I would. I was determined to show up in the world as best as I could. I realized that even if I struggled and continually fell down, somebody was going to get a glimpse of my greatness. So, I focused on the work in front of me. I consistently fought through the clouds of doubt. Lord knows I struggled. I went to therapy. I drank my water and prayed. I was working on myself like never before to get well inside and out.

Daily, I strived to follow directions to produce a great work product. I learned how to coach students through the FSU coaching model. Patience really was a virtue. I called out to the Lord for help daily, especially on my breaks between coaching students. I needed the struggles to dissipate.

During that season, I asked myself how it was possible for my thorns to still hold me back when I had just found my calling. It wasn't fair. Where was God?! Then, I thought back to the parable of the lame man. I imagined that if Jesus was talking directly to me, he would ask me, "So, do you want to be healed or not, Felicia?" I decided that I wanted to be healed, and one night, I decided to tell Him.

"Dear Lord, yes, I want to be healed. So, what do I need to do?"

That night, I had a dream. I was walking somewhere and it was very foggy. I couldn't see anything. Suddenly, a precious voice sang, "Felicia, it's time for Beautiful Healing." The voice was faint, yet audible. Was it Mama? I heard it again. This time, it was a bit stronger and filled with joy.

"Oh, Felicia, it's time for Beautiful Healing!"

Then, I woke up. I propped myself up on the pillows and acknowledged that this was the Lord at work. I couldn't let myself miss what He was revealing to me right then and there.

He had answered my prayer. The dream revealed:
- It was time for me to start walking
- Each step of my life had a purpose
- Beautiful Healing

He had always guided me throughout my life, even if I didn't know where I was going. Therefore, I needed to trust that He would continually guide me.

I prayed for the strength to be obedient and progress faithfully.

Just as doubt would have it, I realized that I didn't have a lot of specifics. Even though the vision was vivid, what did God really mean? The Lord had provided more than enough information. I didn't really believe He had, though—at least, not at first.

It only took a few hours after the dream for me to overthink things. For example, I asked myself, Will I be well enough to walk this path of Beautiful Healing? Will I be smart enough when I get to wherever the Lord wants me to go? The questions bubbled up. Memories of failure flooded my mind. Then, I realized I was just like the man on the mat. When Jesus asked him if he wanted to be healed, he said, "But no one put me in the water!" He deflected the attention away from himself by focusing on other things and blaming other people. Here I was with all of these questions for God, like "Where am I going to find insurance?" and "Who is going to hire me to work part-time?" The Lord didn't mention all that in my dream. I was afraid of stepping out.

12 years prior, I had a vision of a ministry called Beautiful Healing. I saw this organization providing a number of unique experiences designed to unveil authentic beauty and introduce how healing occurs over a lifetime. I remembered the signs the Lord had shown me over the course of those 12 years. There were so many signs. So many. I couldn't possibly continue to deny them. I decided I would pick up my mat and trust God. I wouldn't waste another minute battling with indecision. The sacrifice Jesus made for me was so much larger than any excuse. It was time.

I didn't know how exactly to maneuver my path at first, but later that week, a light bulb went off while I was writing in my journal. I put pen to paper and experienced a breakthrough. I recalled how the Lord ordered my steps and led me to the ever-so-nurturing Life Coaching Center, a place where I discovered my purpose by empowering students. I learned that it was not a sin to love myself just how God made me. I will never forget the day when my supervisor equipped me to seek coaching at the Adult Learning and Education Center on campus. You see, for years, I struggled with being on time, staying organized, and making critical decisions. I always wondered if something was wrong with me. It was easy to stay in denial. Well, I finally faced the fear. Life coaching was something that I was really good at. I was willing to get on the other side of "this" because nothing would hold me back from doing what I loved. Therefore, I took the test and learned that I had ADHD. I realized that I could sharpen my executive functioning skills like time management and focus. It was okay that I had ADHD. With the permission of my supervisor, I was cleared to attend weekly coaching sessions for this diagnosis. The Lord had made a way! I was all in.

With every session, my confidence grew. It took me a while, but I decided that ADHD would not define me; life coaching taught me that. It was okay to be a real person with real struggles. I didn't have to be perfect. I wasn't alone anymore. I had people in my life who I could relate to, gracious souls that shared my burden when I didn't feel good, made mistakes, and felt ashamed. I learned to recognize my inner strength, beauty, and intelligence. I learned that celebrating myself was a great thing to do. I didn't have to wait until I was perfect because I never would be! When the time came for me to depart the Life Coaching Center, I was equipped with a renewed mindset. That certainly sounds like a lot of healing to me!

Clearly, the light of Christ emboldened every experience at the Life Coaching Center at FSU. I trusted the Lord with no hesitation. I was no longer a slave to fear. I was a child of God!

With newfound strength, I confidently sat tall. Soon after, I mustered to my knees. With mat in hand, I stood up. The desire to obey the Lord was worth standing for! I was ready. Sis, you may have been on a mat for a long time in your life. Years, even. Look at the lame man—38 years. However, you, too, have an opportunity to get up. Are you willing? The act of picking up my mat meant that I had a decision to make! Once ill, yet no longer. I asked the Lord to direct my steps and He didn't fail me. I peacefully walked out of the Life Coaching Center with a transformed heart, healed from bitter grief. I was a kinder, softer, and more present woman who no longer hid in the shadows.

On January 4, 2019, with my mat in hand, I took my first step down the unknown path of Beautiful Healing. It was time to embrace the light.

The Supernatural

Can you remember a time when you felt really happy deep inside? Girl, let me tell you something. I like to go walking at Lake Ella in the mornings—not too early, now, because that's not how I roll. I head there before it gets too hot. I like the shade. When I step out of my car, I like the feeling of the sun—only for a minute or two, though, because I like the shade better. Well, one morning, the sun was just beaming! I felt like something was truly different. The only way that I can describe it is that I felt like a part of me was finally able to breathe. With every fiber of my being, I felt that I was made new in Christ. Just like that! Wow.

I took what felt like the deepest breath of my life and wondered what had just happened. I heard a small voice say, "Felicia, I want to introduce you to a fresh peace, the kind that is only available on the other side of tragedy." Well, hello, peace, I thought. Amen!

After that supernatural encounter, I retreated within. The Lord pulled me closer to Him. I didn't resist this time. You see, I had been seeking Him all throughout my unraveling season, and just like that, He spoke to me. The next two months were spent getting lost in the word of God. As I found Him, He found me. I was falling in love with my Creator; this was the greatest love I had ever known!

In essence, the Lord prepared a soft place, a haven, for me to come to terms with all that remained: myself, my heartbreaks, and my disappointments.

I rescheduled chat sessions with friends and took Jesus with me to the coffee shop. Yes, Lord. We needed to talk and talk some more. I purposely muted the world as I scooted closer and closer to the Lord. I had heard enough of what other people had to say; my mind was aligned with the Holy Spirit. Give me more God! More of the light! Truth! That's ALL I had on my mind. I lost track of time playing outdoors, too. The flowers were brighter. The sun shined beautifully. Everywhere I looked, I saw new life; beautiful, fresh life. My soul was breathing again. No more anxiety. Glory!

The Fountain of Forgiveness

As Louis was heading to work one morning, he said, "Babe, you look different. I can see peace all over you. What's new?"

"I don't know what you see, but I have been spending more time in the Word," I responded, grinning. He smiled and we kissed. Muah!

Later that day, I felt compelled to go enjoy some more nature. I was drawn to a lovely fountain in the center of the lake that I had begun to frequent. Peace was all around. Then, I realized that I could be free just like the water in the fountain. All I had to do was forgive some people, starting with myself. Vivid memories began to unfold. It was happening again—another supernatural experience.

The only way that I can describe it is that I knew specifically what I was supposed to forgive myself for, even though I wasn't actively thinking about it. I call this a download from Heaven. I saw how all the self-inflicted pain from years of negative self-talk had beaten me down. Healing came over me as tears began to fall. It was time I handled my own heart with care. As I continued to forgive myself, the memories kept coming. The stubborn knots were untangling. I prayed and forgave myself for falling short at times, blaming myself for other people's issues, and believing that I would never amount to anything. I released the haunting guilt of not being well or strong enough to do more for Mama in her last days. Listen to me, sis. No matter how long pain has taken space in your heart, forgiveness clears the clutter, allowing an ocean of precious healing to rush in. As a memory from college surfaced, more healing tears began to rush from my eyes.

The Party

While attending Valdosta State University, I met a young woman at a Bible study on campus. She was also from a small town and we bonded over our love for Jesus. We both also loved shopping at the Christian bookstore and connected very naturally. After the next Bible study, she invited me to her birthday party. I accepted her invitation, even though I wasn't really experienced with going to birthday parties and often kept to myself. Maybe it was because of my limited understanding of socializing, as I didn't get out much as a teenager. My new friend and I browsed around the mall and discussed outfits and new music. I felt really comfortable talking to her. I felt… accepted. This was new! After meeting her, I decided that college life wasn't so bad. The day before the party, she called me and asked me what color I was going to wear. Even though I was feeling a bit uneasy about the party, I told her I would wear my pink blouse. "Me, too," she said. That was also her favorite color. I smiled wide. I had a friend! Yay!

While getting ready, I listened to Destiny's Child and smiled at myself in the mirror. I felt cute. Then, I started laughing. Was this what fun felt like? Yeah, it was! After I got into my truck, I referred to my MapQuest directions to get to the party. I adjusted the air conditioning vent towards my perspiring face. It wasn't even that hot outside. I must have just been excited. It was okay. After I put the truck in park, I grabbed some napkins to wipe my face. Then, I looked in the mirror and I began to feel down. It was happening again, and the sad truth was that "it" had happened twice before. I felt like I was struggling with something, but didn't know what it was. Tears welled up in my eyes. Discouraged, I wiped them away. Honestly, I knew that I was taking a chance by making plans with my friend. I was taking a chance by getting my hopes up. I really liked her. I also liked being liked by others. I would really try to go inside this time. Maybe, just maybe, I could feel strong enough to go inside this time. I remained in the truck for another couple of minutes. The negative thoughts crept in slowly. Why did I even come to this? My chest tightened and my hands felt cold. If my friend knew that my struggle was like this, she might not even want me to be at her party.

I placed my face in my hands and started to cry. I kept tissues in my glove compartment because I tended to cry a lot. I never understood why I cried so much, though. The brawl between depression and anxiety had begun. The emotional beatdown was in full effect in my heart.

Feeling paralyzed, I turned the ignition and drove out of the yard. I texted my friend to tell her that I couldn't make it.
"Aw! Why not?" She responded. "I thought I saw your truck, girl. I was so excited to see you, Felicia!"

"I was excited to see you, too, friend. I think I have a stomach bug or something," I replied after clearing my throat. My left hand trembled as tears dripped from my chin. I held the phone loosely. Yet again, I felt like such a loser.

My heart desperately wanted to turn around and go celebrate with my friend, yet that strong inner tug pulled me towards my bed. I felt completely exhausted. Once again, "it" won. Once again, I got into my bed and turned off all the lights. Once again, I hadn't made it to the party.

I would be lying if I said I never thought about that night. After all these years, that memory still hurts. Sometimes, I wonder if that friend and I would still be in contact today if I had been well.

While still facing the fountain, I forgave myself for not knowing what I now know. I hadn't known that these subtle and mysterious feelings had names: Depression and Anxiety. I forgave myself for not knowing that treatment was available. I forgave myself for the self-hatred I practiced when I couldn't articulate how I felt inside. I didn't understand how to express those moments. I was so ashamed. I forgave myself that day, though. I let all the grief from the memory fade. I imagined it getting washed away in a large wave at the beach. Feeling a lot lighter, tears of healing replaced all those tears of agony I had cried as a young woman. I wiped my face and turned on my favorite song by CeCe Winans. I knew it would help me embrace this newfound release. This peace was precious. It was all mine. Before I left the lake, I asked the Lord to forgive me for:

- Every offense I had ever taken against others
- The anger I felt towards God after Mama died
- Lack of strength
- Selfishness
- Shame
- Everything that I had not understood that had caused much agony over the course of my life.

It clicked. I didn't have to work so hard anymore. In fact, I never had to… I just hadn't known any better. I lifted my empty hands and rested in praising the Lord freely.

Sis, take a moment to imagine what it would feel like to let go of the things that gnaw at your peace. How would it feel to release all of the joy stealers and soul grabbers—grudges, anger, fear, and pain? Your soul just may catch its breath, too!

Acknowledgment + Forgiveness = Emotional Freedom

Walking around with empty hands feels good, sis. Care to join me?

Ever So Grateful,
Felicia

Prayer

Sis, I pray that the closed regions of your heart open and make room for healing to flow to the seat of your soul. I hope you laugh out loud unabashedly, smile genuinely, and embrace what matters most in life. You are free. I pray that unconditional love greets you in the morning sunrise and that every cell in your body releases toxins, pain, and hurt. You are healthy. You matter. You are seen. You are worthy of the absolute best.

1. _How do you feel after reading love letter 2?_

NOTE TO
SELF

2. _What do you need to let go of?_

3. What limiting beliefs have prevented you from releasing

baggage?

_____

_____

_____

_____

_____

_____

_____

_____

_____

_____

_____

_____

4. What might your life look and feel like after you let go of what you listed in question 2?

_____

_____

_____

_____

_____

_____

_____

_____

_____

_____

_____

_____

5. *Write down any emotions or lingering thoughts you have about*

this book so far.

_____

_____

_____

_____

_____

_____

_____

_____

_____

_____

Love Letter 3
Love

Dear Sis,

At around age 25, I recall impatiently asking God, "Where is my husband already?!" I was so tired of being single. Being patient and waiting was not for me. A sista needed guidance. Since God was not answering my prayers fast enough, I decided to see life's delays as a green light to "do me." I sat my morals and values aside because it was time to live, baby! Sis, this is precisely how misalignment sneaks in. I was in a rut. I wasn't getting any younger, and I had begun to feel societal pressure to get married. Family consistently started asking me, "Felicia, when are you getting married? You aren't getting any younger." Ugh! I was so sick of the mess. The man has to show up first, y'all, I thought.

Instead of calling a strong woman of God for counsel (I assured myself that she was not going to understand), I chose to figure this out on my own. I developed a sarcastic attitude with other Christians, pretty much labeling them all as fake. I knew I was falling by the wayside in my faith and I wasn't proud of my behavior. I also knew that the real reason I didn't want to call my mentor was because she was a great believer. She would tell me to wait on the Lord regarding my future husband. I didn't want to hear that, though. I vaguely remembered my Precious Moments Bible and wondered if I would ever have that childlike trust in the Lord. The truth was, I didn't understand how to "adult" and obey God when it came to the idea of marriage. As frustration built, I admitted that I was lost. I realized that the wise believers from my childhood church, who I often referred to as the "elder saints," really knew what they were talking about. Those sweet people were not fake. They had what I longed for—faith. Feeling convicted, I knew the time had come to make some changes in my life. I chose to repent, which means that I acknowledged my behavior, and I disagreed with it. I had strayed away from the Lord. I didn't feel condemned. I felt convicted. I missed the sweet fellowship with my Savior. I knew that He loved me. I just wanted to have a boo, too. A boo that was okay with not following all the rules. I wanted to fornicate. I wanted that boo to hurry up and find me. My breakthrough moment came when I made peace with God. I laid all my ideas down and asked the Lord for strength to help me wait on my husband, which I knew would be His absolute best for me. I returned to the Bible study group the following week. I intentionally turned back to God. I abandoned the long route and rediscovered His word. His directions were just better. I started praying for the man who God created for me. Any kind of man just wouldn't do! I wanted the one the Lord had in mind when He made me; my Boaz. I was finally willing to wait. I had learned that I was a daughter of the King. The Lord had a plan, and I embraced that His plans would be way better than mine. I was grateful to have renewed faith again.

Want to hear a love story, sis? I met a young man by the name of Louis Dilbert in 2006. This very tall, dark, handsome, and clean-cut man happened to work down the hall from me. One morning, he stopped by my office. "Well, well! Good morning!" Okay, so he was a morning person. Playing it cool, I said hello. He had this big smile on his face. He wanted to know where I was from, how long I had been working for the university, if I had any siblings, what church I went to… he was a talker. I attempted to be kind, but didn't make much eye contact with him. I was shy and nursing a broken heart. I decided that ALL men were toxic. So, brotha could calm down with all that humor and friendliness. My heart was off-limits.

Well, Louis continually ignored and laughed at my attempts at making poker faces. He boldly invited me to lunch out of the blue the following week. I made it clear that this lunch would be just lunch, nothing more, and that I would gladly pay for my own meal. He agreed nonchalantly. I was surprised at his response—not because I expected him to pay for my meal, but because he didn't seem to care that I was trying to scare him away. He wasn't disrespectful. He was confident, and that was attractive. Not long after we were seated at the restaurant, Louis made me laugh! I couldn't even deny it; he was hilarious. He reminded me a lot of my brother. During that lunch, I decided that Louis would go from being off-limits to being in the "friend zone." He was a good guy; however, my heart was still off-limits! Well, Louis and I began to take long walks through friendship (seven years, to be exact). Louis was different. He talked about his love for God and family. He adored his mother and sisters.

This man was content walking beside me and holding my hand respectfully. And, sis, he knew he was in the friend zone! He was simply refreshing. Six months later, on what seemed like the hottest day in Florida, I went to grab some lunch. When I returned to my car, I noticed my tire was flat. Not today, Satan, I thought. I needed to get back to work for an important meeting in less than two hours. I was hesitant to call Louis because I didn't want him to think I was desperate. However, I didn't know what to do, so I called him and asked for his advice—not his help.

"Hey, Felicia! Where are you exactly? I'm on my lunch break, too. How about this, I'm coming over there to change it. I'm on my way now," he said. Sis, Louis showed up in a full suit with that big smile. "I've got this," he assured me. I looked on with awe as his tall self got under that car and changed that tire with the quickness—all while wearing that suit. When he got up off the ground, I couldn't help but notice how fine he was. Lou had been in the gym!

"Okay, you are ready to roll! Call me when you get back to work, please." Then, he flashed that big smile. I turned my head as I blushed. I couldn't help but notice that he was always caring for my well-being. I remember when he asked if he could court me. I always knew he was special. I remember my grandma Ossie Bell telling me that any man who mentions the word "court" is a good man! We walked through a pure courtship and then entered engagement.

Oh, how Louis cherished me. His kind ways softened my heart. Sis, I wrote the following love letter to my husband for our sixth anniversary:

Dear my Louis,

After marriage, I had some trouble with submitting to you. I was in unfamiliar territory. Please forgive me for pushing you away. I'll admit I have wanted to get married for a long time. I prayed for a husband for years. However, I didn't pray about the submission part. Louis, I thought submission was another word for slavery! As you know, I have experienced a pattern of running from things I don't understand. But, babe, I didn't expect you to run after me. I had no clue just how much you love God! The further I ran, the more you chased me! And when you caught me, you loved the hellish ignorance out of me. You taught me about my foolish ways with the most beautiful heart, demonstrating the love of Christ. Louis, your loyalty to Christ ushered me back into the arms of Jesus. You were patient as I learned how to love the Lord, me, and you. I sometimes forget how hard I prayed for a great husband, and you have been more than I could have ever imagined. I couldn't have made it through the loss of Mama without you. When the storms of sickness knocked me off my feet, you didn't hesitate to sit down next to me. Then, you held my hand even tighter and prayed when I couldn't say a word. When the hurricane of grief stirred all around, you grabbed me and hid me as best you could. When the sun came out after the rain, you held my head up towards the light. You still made me smile when absolutely nothing was funny. And, Hallelujah, when I picked up my mat and began to walk again... you praised with me, never doubting God's will for my life! Oh, I couldn't bear this long, long walk without you. You love me, thorns and all. I'm honored to hold your hand as we continue to walk, my Lou Lou. One day, I confidently know that our little ones will join us in our walk (yay!). In the meantime, there is no other man who can hold my hand as you can. Let's keep walking, Louis Lawrence Dilbert. I adore you. Happy Anniversary!

With so much love,
Mrs. Felicia Dilbert

Louis and Felicia Dilbert, 2020
Cynecia Manning/ necieDIMPLE

Jesus led Louis to me. Sis, the Lord can lead your husband to you, too.
Believe me.

A Mother's Love

In 2013, I learned about the Florida State University Center for Life Coaching. I worked at Tallahassee Community College. I remember chatting with Mama in the kitchen on a regular day after work. She cooked the chicken and I talked. Dang, I should have taken notes on that recipe! As she turned the chicken, I told her that I wanted to be a Life Coach.

"You know, Esha, there will come a day when you will do that. You would be perfect for that," she told me. "Okay, I want you to pinky promise me right now that when that life coaching job comes along, you will apply for it—no matter what! Girl, do you hear me? No matter what, you will apply, you will get the job, and you will be an excellent Life Coach, Esha!"

"Okay, Mama!"

We laughed, hugged, and pinky promised. And all was well. Two months after Mama's passing, I saw a job advertisement for a full-time life coaching opportunity at Florida State University. Here was that job opportunity Mama referenced in the kitchen that day. Now, God, why did the best opportunity manifest at the worst possible time in my life? I was barely able to get out of bed on most days.

Love Sat Next to Me

I told Louis about the job opportunity, and, naturally, he encouraged me to apply. The thing was, I didn't have the strength to apply. I just wanted to sleep. I was in and out of therapy, still grieving terribly. I will never forget how my precious husband came home after work and asked me to join him at the kitchen table. He said, "Babe, if I have to watch you type in every word on this application, I will. You are perfect for this job! You've got to apply." Louis sat there with me. He reassured me when I got frustrated. My sweet husband encouraged me as I sifted through old files to locate the exact dates of my past job history. I felt so defeated. With waning motivation, I somehow continued to complete the application. Louis has a way of gently encouraging me during sad times. He quietly reminded me of the promise I made to Mama. I did pinky promise her, after all.

Love encourages you to press forward when you are tapped out. Love sits right there with you, talks to you, and whispers to you that you can still do it while reminding you what you are made of. With Louis by my side, I applied for the job at 11:58 p.m., two minutes shy of the deadline. I did it!

God's Love

As Mama's health declined in March of 2017, I specifically prayed for the Lord to send clear directions to prepare me for my last days with her. One afternoon, I suddenly had trouble breathing while driving on the interstate. I managed to park my car on the side of the road and began to pray between sobs. I could feel my chest tightening and immediately knew that I was having a panic attack. To ease my anxiety, I played "You're So Holy" by Cece Winans.

Thankfully, I recovered within minutes. Then, my phone rang; it was a friend.

"Hi, Felicia! What are you up to?"

"I'm hanging in there, girl," I replied sluggishly.

"Just hanging in there? Meet me for lunch today at the Italian spot. Let's spend some time together. I miss you, friend," she said.

Gosh, it felt so lovely to be thought of. How did my friend know to call me at that exact moment, though? I could not deny that the Lord put my name on that woman's heart, and she willingly listened by picking up the phone and calling me. The Lord was working through my friend on my behalf. Over lunch, she spoke about the loss of her mother due to non-small cell lung cancer, which caused my mother's decline. She generously provided specific details about how she endured her mother's final days. My answer to prayer was sitting right in front of me. If I ever doubted God, I quit doubting that day. My Lord cared so much for me that He answered my agonizing prayer on a challenging day. What if I had allowed that panic attack to keep me from answering the phone? I would have missed my miraculous answer to prayer. I thought about how Jeremiah 1:5 says, "Before I shaped you in the womb, I knew all about you. Before you saw the light of day, I had holy plans for you: a prophet to the nations—that's what I had in mind for you." Jesus ordained that divine appointment over dinner for such a time as that. As I said my prayers that night, I asked the Lord to instill within me the kind of boldness that my friend had. I wanted to be like her. I committed to always express prophetic words from the Lord. Why hold back?

That day, I was reminded that the Lord uses willing people to deliver His truth. He relies on willing and obedient vessels to carry out His plan. My spirit was overflowing from the wisdom, love, and compassion that my friend delivered to me. She was so real with me. We sat there and cried after we ate our dinner. Death hurts, sis, but the Lord will not leave you to suffer alone. He sent my friend that day, and on this day, He has sent me to share this letter with you. Allow the truth to sit within your heart. Sis, the Lord is mindful of you! Yes, you. Deuteronomy 31:8 reads, "Do not be afraid or discouraged, for the LORD will personally go ahead of you. He will be with you; He will neither fail you nor abandon you." When our dinner ended, I hugged my friend and headed out to my car. I hadn't felt so light in months. Now, this was peace. I got in my car and just smiled. Thank you, Lord. My breathing had settled. I had witnessed a miracle. As I drove out of the parking lot, I headed to see my Mama, equipped with confidence. I now knew how to face precious moments ahead. Thank you, Jesus!

I lost count of all the miracles that took place in that season. Every single day, the Lord sent love letters through people who were willing to speak life into my heart. Words of hope, faith, love. Words in DUE season, too. Each time I felt overwhelmed by grief, a fresh and present helper arrived to resuscitate me. Although it took me a while to breathe again, I was revived. One night, my faith quelled. I wondered if the Lord was even real. Not even two minutes later, I received a text from a close friend, asking if she could call and pray. Yet again, the Lord had sent another willing vessel to douse the flames of disbelief. The Lord was real!

When the fires of depression raged, the Lord laid me on the heart of a strong woman of God who I had not spoken to in years. She randomly called me one morning. I was in bed. The depression was so massive, all I could manage was just to lay there. "Felicia, you have been on my mind all morning. How are you, sis? I can hear it in your voice. You alright? May I pray for you right now? I kept feeling this tugging in my heart to call you, and I am so glad I did," she said with a firm voice. Tears rolled down my face as I listened to her sweet voice pray. Yet again, the Lord sent support. I realize now that nothing about that call was random. My spirit was lifting. As she continued to pray, I sat straight up in bed. Wow!

These supernatural occurrences of powerful prayer and fervent faith extinguished threats from the enemy. One night, I dreamed that when people pray in the name of Jesus, the power of prayer quenches flames of unbelief. Moment of transparency—I honestly never believed the Lord would come through for me like this. I prayed differently this season, though. I drew closer to Him with everything in me. I pursued Jesus. As my heart broke from loss, illness, and confusion, my faith skyrocketed.

Timeless Love

I believe the Lord has a sense of humor—boy, was I in for a surprise. While sorting through a box in my new office, a picture of Mama and I caught my eye. The Panama City Beach trip! Oh, man, we loved the beach! Giddy, I picked up the frame and hugged it! This was it!

Mom and I
Panama City Beach, 2010

You see, up until that moment, I didn't know how to decorate my new office. Mom was the one who loved decorating. Well, now I had to figure this out on my own.

I decided that my space would be filled with tranquility. Everyone who entered my office would feel the calm energy, including myself. With every seashell, starfish, and fishnet wall hanging, I dedicated the space to that memory of Mama and I; two fun chicks just chillin' at the beach on a hot summer day. It only took one glimpse at love to give me what I was longing for: harmony. Even in a season of misalignment, I was healing.

Here's to Healing,
Felicia

NOTE TO
SELF

1. *How do you feel about love letter 3?*

2. Can you relate to Felicia's impatience at the beginning of the letter? How so?

_____

_____

_____

_____

_____

_____

_____

_____

_____

_____

_____

NOTE TO
SELF

3. _How have you handled pressure from others regarding_

relationships, starting a family or achieving a degree?

4. Have you ever turned your back on God?

What did that process feel like? Dig deep here. Take your time.

_____

_____

_____

_____

_____

_____

_____

_____

_____

_____

_____

5. In your opinion, how can you cultivate more patience in your
life?

_____

_____

_____

_____

_____

_____

_____

_____

_____

_____

_____

Love Letter 4
Truth

Sis,

Honesty is a prerequisite to healing.

Check-In

     A check-in is defined as taking the time to tell yourself the truth. Taking time to reflect is valuable and crucial. Whether daily, weekly, biweekly, or monthly, I encourage you to make space to develop a reflection routine. Everyone else sees and perceives you, so why not check in with yourself every now and then? You are worth it!

     I make space on a monthly basis to reflect on spiritual, financial, physical, mental, and relational aspects of my life. When I am doing a physical check-in, I pick up my journal and go to my cozy spot (I encourage you to do the same) to focus. I flow from questions to statements and go back to questions sometimes, always doing what feels good to me in the moment. I want my check-in to flow easily and feel light. My check-ins consist of me answering healthy questions like, "Where am I holding tension in my body?" and "Am I breathing calmly?" As well as taking these steps:

- I identify what is on my mind.
- I stretch.
- I do a little dance.
- I play an intentional song that encourages me. I listen to Tweet's "I Was Created for This" on repeat. This step is especially helpful when I'm doubting something.

Next up is my emotional check-in:

- How am I showing up in the world?
- Do I have any unresolved concerns that are bothering me?
- Have I said everything I needed to say today? This week?
- Am I carrying any resentment towards myself or others?

     Then, I prioritize my next steps. I face what I need to face. I write answers down. Don't skip that part. Addressing what you are feeling is a healing behavior, sis! It works. The more honest you are, the more you will grow. Hone in. Freedom is on the other side of telling the truth, so get after it. I conclude my check-in by listing action steps. I commit to reading the action steps during the following week. I challenge myself to meet the standards I set. I remind myself to be graceful with my spirit when I fall short, too.

Essentially, a check-in means making the time to create space to face the whole truth about yourself.

The Power of Truth

As a young girl, I dreamed of following in my father's footsteps of entrepreneurship. I wanted to own a business. Regardless of all my challenges, deep in my heart, I wanted to achieve this goal.

After leaving my job at FSU, the plan was to acquire a part-time job to serve as a financial buffer before jumping into full-time entrepreneurship. I didn't know what my future held. A part-time job just made sense because it would help me transition from working full-time, right? I decided to apply for a position at a non-profit. It wouldn't hurt to put my name in the hat. After all, the job title was cool.

I entered the job interview with confidence. However, I had an undeniable feeling that the job wasn't quite what I was looking for. After the interview, I knew my gut was right. No matter how nice the idea of part-time job security sounded, I listened to my discernment. Even though I had no clue how I would supplement my income, I believed in myself. After a week or so, administrative staff called me to inform me that I did not get the position.

"You may not believe this; however, I wasn't going to take the job if you offered it to me," I boldly said.

We both laughed hysterically! I savored the brilliance of my boldness, all the while asking myself if I had really just said that out loud! Nonetheless, an amazing conversation ensued and a deeper authentic connection was established—all from telling the truth.

Later that month, the staff member and I continued to engage in dialogue about passion and purpose. I chose faith over fear. After much prayer, Louis gave me his blessing to begin renting my first office for my personal development business, Beautiful Healing. My Lord, I was so happy! My dream of providing tools for women to unlearn unworthiness unapologetically was coming true. All I could do was smile!

Prayers of Truth

My grandma, Ossie Bell, took prayer time very seriously. She absolutely loved to pray. I remember her praying, "Father in Heaven and all of the angels, I love you and I come to you as humbly as I know how." I was seven years old when I joined her during prayer time.

Grandma would lay two pillows on the floor on the left side of the bed for us to kneel on. "We've got to be comfortable because we are going to be praying for a long time," she would say.

I was happy to pray with her. Everything about her was alright with me. She was never in a rush around prayer time because she laid all her troubles down in prayer. I liked the idea of that.

I sensed that the Holy Bible held the keys to what we prayed about every day. It was a source with specific directions. I loved the intention in her voice as she read the Bible. I also sensed that Jesus was our Heavenly Father and he loved us all very much. He was powerful and not to be played with. Grandma and I were taking part in a very important task each morning when we prayed. This was a respectable honor.

I soon volunteered to pray for each family member as they walked by grandma's room to enter the kitchen. Since we prayed early in the morning, Daddy was the first one to walk by. I will never forget the way his work boots sounded hitting the floor. I prayed for him to enjoy breakfast and have a good work day. Soon after, I would hear Mama pass by carrying my little brother. I would get up and go kiss him on the cheek between "amen"s. Lastly, grandma would conclude prayer time by recognizing all national leadership officials, family members up north, friends and family from church, and everyone who lived on Old Camilla Road. She loved everybody! She was right about those pillows—we definitely prayed for a long while. Over the years, I fell in love with prayer. It still is the wisest choice I make every day.

Beautiful Truth

My grandmother's eyes were black with a hint of blue circling them and she had the most beautiful salt-and-pepper hair. She had a big laugh and an even bigger smile. She served her church faithfully and enjoyed talking. She loved people, and people loved her right back. I remember watching soap operas—we called them "stories"—with her on the rare occasions that I did not go to school. It was such a joy to be around her. She was not only my grandma, but also my friend. The most impactful lesson I learned from her was to always tell the truth.

The Skinny on Development

One evening in 2019, I found an old photo that had been taken at least 15 years prior. Seeing it triggered me. Negative feelings rushed in. I was at least 100 pounds lighter then. I looked like a model. I started to feel bad because I don't look like that anymore. Slowly, I remembered what I had dealt with back then, though. My mind became clear as I was reminded of what laid beneath the surface in that beautiful picture. Yes, I was younger and my features reflected that. However, the camera did not capture my insecurities. Everything wasn't perfect in that picture. I remembered the whole backstory while standing there looking at my younger self. Even still, I decided to pursue healing regarding self-image. Taking authority over my emotions was the goal. In Genesis 1:27, the Word reveals, "I am made in His image." I took the verse personally and I repeated it daily until it was at the forefront of my mind. Who was I to argue with the way God created me? I now recognize the power of God's word. I received wisdom that reflects truth, strength, and peace from that one verse. As the years pass, we women must refresh our way of thinking about our younger selves.

I am grateful that I am doing much a better job of accepting myself and loving myself as Christ has created me.

Spontaneous Reflection Time

Sis, take this time as an invitation to rest your mind. Allow space

between your thoughts and express yourself.
Consider the way you live. Are you comfortable?
What needs to change?
What are you tired of going through? When did it start?

Difficult Truth

"Be anxious for nothing, but in everything by prayer and supplication, with thanksgiving, let your requests be made known to God; 7 and the peace of God, which surpasses all understanding, will guard your hearts and minds through Christ Jesus." Philippians 4:6-7.

I have struggled with anxiety and depression for the majority of my adult life. The first time I noticed it was in college. I remember waiting until everyone exited the dining hall before walking in to get my dinner. I knew the hall closed at 8:00 p.m., so if I went at 7:45 p.m., I could literally run in and out without having to interact with people. I was so afraid of people and I didn't know why, but I knew something wasn't quite right with this fear I was experiencing. I remember thinking, Is something wrong with me?

Over the years, I often contemplated going to talk to a therapist. When I told a couple of people about my interest in seeking help, I was told that only crazy people go to therapy and that it would be a complete waste of money. "Have you really prayed about this, Felicia? Honey, anoint your head with oil and cast the spirit of depression out of yourself! Why would you go to see a therapist?" Heeding their advice, I decided not to seek professional help. My life became a sadder and sadder experience. The hole I perceived myself to be in became deeper and deeper, and I always felt sad. I felt like I was on an emotional roller coaster ride that would never end. I would be excited to participate in social events, but then lose all motivation minutes beforehand. I began to withdraw from talks with Mama. I would cancel plans with friends. Another three years passed, and as an adult, things had changed as expected over the years. One pattern remained the same: depression. I should have gone to see a therapist. This heavy, heavy burden brought me to a lower place. My spirit was broken by the sadness. One night in my little apartment, I cried out to Jesus to help me. I prayed harder than I ever had before.

The next day, the Holy Spirit led me to call a friend. I had no idea what I was supposed to say if she answered my call. When she answered the phone, I courageously said, "Sister, I am in trouble. Please help me!" She guided me to calm down. Her voice was so soothing. I explained what was going on. She listened graciously.

Then, she gave me a local doctor's (let's call her Dr. A) contact information. She mentioned that her husband dealt with similar challenges and his life changed once he sought professional help. Her word choice and voice inflection were so disarming. She was the first person who spoke positively about seeing a therapist. I thought she might have been lying to me. I could feel her empathetic heart, though. I am so glad the Lord laid her on my heart. I knew I was supposed to call her. Within the next two weeks, I found the courage to call Dr. A. Unfortunately, Dr. A was booked for the next several months and didn't accept my insurance coverage, but I didn't let that stop me. I decided to schedule an appointment to see a different counselor until I could afford to see Dr. A. I continued counseling for several sessions and noticed intermittent progress. I soon noticed that I experienced less stress and more peace. It wasn't long before I began to notice a pattern to my feelings of depression. I realized I struggled more with depression during harder seasons of life, such as when experiencing physical illnesses or frustrations at work. During those periods, I began to seek more medical assistance.

Sis, there will be obstacles on your path of Beautiful Healing. You have to decide that you won't give up, regardless of the minor roadblocks. Even though I didn't have the preferred insurance, I didn't let that stop me from pursuing complete healing. I called Dr. A's office and inquired about the out-of-pocket cost. I figured I could save enough coins to go to Dr. A. How much could it be? Well, I was wrong. It was expensive! I felt like cursing. It seemed like I couldn't get a break. All I wanted was to feel better!

After a long year, I got a new job, and lo and behold, they offered me the exact insurance that Dr. A's office accepted. Even though I was having more good days than bad, I still called to make an appointment once the insurance kicked in. The receptionist said that the earliest Dr. A could see me was at the end of the following month. Even though that was roughly seven weeks away, I decided to look on the bright side. I had waited an entire year to become a patient, so what was another seven weeks?

The first time I met the doctor, I could instantly tell that I was in the right place. I felt safe, like all the waiting had been worth it. Dr.

A possessed all the great attributes from each of the counselors I had previously seen. Glory! Yes, I made it to the right one!

With every appointment, the tumultuous beatdowns of depression calmed. I was hungry to learn. So, this is what this "thing" is called. The chemical imbalances, moodiness, and dark clouds were all synonymous with "it." Therapy gave me the depth of understanding I had been seeking for years. All of this was not just about a "broken me." The mind gets sick just like the body does. Dr. A was so dope, too. She explained this complex stuff in such a kind way. She didn't fuss at me when I asked the same questions time after time. She educated the trauma inside of me.

After a lot of visits, I met relief. For example, I noticed less tension in my back when I met new people. I started to sit back in chairs. I didn't talk as fast or as much. I liked this new feeling. This was inner peace! Learning about mental health was liberating, powerful, and fascinating all at the same time. During the third appointment, I learned about the benefits of cognitive therapy. I was finally with the right professionally trained practitioner. I could let it ALL out here. THANK YOU, JESUS!!!!!

Hallelujah!
Cynecia Manning/ necieDIMPLE

After my mother died, the sadness was heavy and I was too weak to make it through my days. I also had been diagnosed with Diabetes 2 a day before Mama's funeral. I wasn't feeling good. I spoke with my therapist about it all. She explained several remedies. I chose to come to therapy weekly instead of biweekly. I also decided to try a medication for depression. I was so afraid of going to the pharmacy to pick it up. What will the pharmacist think? Will she judge me? Will she say the name of my prescription out loud in front of all the people in line? Oh, God! I panicked. Well, turns out, she was a gentle woman with a compassionate smile. She was so chill! I left the pharmacy empowered. Baby, I was about to start healing! Not just because of the medicine (although it helped the depression lift quickly!), but because I was showing up for myself, unapologetically. I was thinking for myself. What a beautiful existence.

Listen, I learned that a winning day is any day when I am equipped to carry out my heavenly Father's will, and it's okay if that equipment comes in the form of a pill. I love prayer, my pastor, my professional doctors, and a prescription (if necessary). No shame! I believe every person can benefit from therapy. Sis, take an honest look at your life. If you know you've been struggling with the same patterns all throughout your life, don't hesitate to seek help from a professional. You got this!

Also, we are all human and there will be tough days. You can come back stronger, though. Let it all be well with your soul. The knowledge I gained through therapy couldn't be farther from the advice that the well-meaning, albeit ignorant people told me for years. Think for yourself, sis.

Every heart issue has an origin, a root from which it began to grow. I embraced that it was fine to have professional assistance in uprooting trauma. I could not fight this battle alone. I was no longer in bondage to the well-meaning saints who believed everything could be healed by prayer. My health was now safe in the confidential hands of a professional. I refused to hold myself back from my healing, even if it meant going to see a therapist regularly.

Today, I own my wellness plan and truth, unapologetically. Wellness for Felicia Dilbert consists of a strong relationship with the Lord, clean eating, self-care, exercise, therapy, and a strong support system. It took me a while to become comfortable with all of this, but now I choose to focus on how healthy I am. I can finally embrace all of the light because I am well enough to do so!

Sis, take GOOD care of yourself. Do not let anything hold you back from pursuing your healing. Understand that healing arrives in different forms and, sometimes, in very unexpected ways. Will you be gentle with yourself in order to embrace healing?

Lastly, I appreciate it most when a person respects that my healing is not on their own timeline. This means that it's not on you to witness or facilitate a person's healing. Well-meaning people want to do that. I'm going to be straight-up with you—that ain't well-meaning. Leave people and their healing alone. Love them unconditionally, instead. Let's say your sister sits in her room in the dark for hours. You have always thought it was strange and often give her a hard time about it. But you say you love her. Pro tip: Stop talking to her in a mean tone. Trust me if she could find a way to be well she would! And stop talking about her to other people. Instead, gently ask her if you can come in there and sit with her. In the dark. Then, listen to her. If she doesn't want to talk, then be quiet. Try holding her hand. Give her a genuine smile. A back rub feels good, right? Or just be quiet. This is how well-intention and well-actioned love behaves.

Love your sister.

Love your sister.

Love your sister.

I love you,
Felicia

NOTE TO
SELF

1. _Self-soothing is a huge component of being gentle with oneself._

How can you plan to encourage yourself on the hard days?

_____

_____

_____

_____

_____

_____

_____

_____

_____

_____

_____

_____

2. _Are you avoiding any truth(s)? If so, what are they?_

_____

_____

_____

_____

_____

_____

_____

_____

_____

_____

_____

_____

3. *Why do you think people struggle with telling the truth?*

_____

_____

_____

_____

_____

_____

_____

_____

_____

_____

_____

_____

4. Have you ever turned your back on God?

What did that process feel like? Dig deep here. Take your time.

_____

_____

_____

_____

_____

_____

_____

_____

_____

_____

_____

_____

NOTE TO
SELF

5. What are your takeaways from this letter?

_____

_____

_____

_____

_____

_____

_____

_____

_____

_____

_____

_____

_____

_____

_____

_____

Love Letter 5
Peace

Hi Sis,

When I worked in the beauty industry, skincare brands promised to solve every skin concern through a variety of creams, lotions, anti-aging potions, and other notions! Each brand claimed that their products were magic, filled with miracle-working ingredients. How could a woman choose the right one? These products promised to prevent wrinkles, erase scars, and give that fresh, youthful glow.

While at the beauty counter, I realized that these brands were making millions of dollars by promising women confidence and peace through cosmetics. Isn't that interesting?

"And he arose, and rebuked the wind, and said unto the sea, 'Peace, be still.' And the wind ceased, and there was a great calm."
— Mark 4:39

Girl, wisdom has taught me that the best anti-aging solution is called peace. I used to think that peace could be purchased. Basically, I figured that there was nothing that a little shopping couldn't solve. My philosophy was that buying things was the key to feeling better. I was shopping my heart out way before I even knew what retail therapy was. My Lord!

Thank God for John 14:27, which states, "I am leaving you with a gift—peace of mind and heart. And the peace I give is a gift the world cannot give. So, don't be troubled or afraid. Authentic peace comes from the Lord."

Thank you, Lord, for giving Your daughters the keys to peace.

Authentic Peace

On a gray, foggy morning in Tallahassee, I woke up in a bad mood. After a busy week of travel, back-to-back meetings, and checking on all my friends, I was exhausted. Thankfully, I had a day of beauty ahead of me! My hair appointment was first. Then, a manicure and pedicure. I had been looking forward to this all month. However, all I wanted to do was cancel. Just go, I told myself. You will feel better. Don't cancel.

Nothing feels fresher than a washed, laid, and feathered head of hair! After an hour, I began to look forward to my day, regardless of the lingering mood. I got dressed and headed to get beautified. Unfortunately, I lost track of time again and sped to the salon like a jackrabbit. As I entered the salon doors, I took a deep breath. Ooh, it smelled so good! The smell was enough to minimize my mood a little bit (yes, aromatherapy!). I tried to leave all weariness in the waiting area. The feeling of sadness was sticky, though.

"Your stylist will be right with you, Felicia," said the friendly receptionist. As I saw my stylist, I could tell that she was annoyed by my tardiness. Aw, shoot.

I immediately complimented my stylist on her boots, hoping to deflect attention from my tardiness.

"Thank you, Felicia. They were a gift from my husband. However, you are late again," she replied, "and we have talked about this repeatedly."

Geez. Another failed attempt. Sigh. Listen, another 4 letter word for ADHD is LATE. The truth of the matter was that, yes, I was late, again. One day, I figured out why I was late just about everywhere I went. It wasn't that day though. Also, I really did like her boots! If I knew where she purchased them, I would have bought them that same day. Oh, the joys of ADHD.

I longed for my stylist's stress-free stride. Shame engulfed me. The reality of my shortcomings added to my inner discomfort.
Deep down, I now secretly wished I had her cute boots and carefree attitude.

She assessed my hair, attached the smock, and invited me to the shampoo bowl with a concerned look on her face.
"Felicia, what's wrong?"

Focusing on the candle flame, I felt myself coming undone. I silently laid back in the chair while a train of tears trickled from the corners of my eyes. My secret was out. My pain dripped down my face.

I wiped my eyes. When I sat up, my stylist invited me to a private hallway and embraced me in a sisterly bear hug. My soul released a sigh of relief.

She looked into my eyes and asked me to tell her what was bothering me. I didn't want to risk judgment, so I said nothing. Thankfully, she asked me again. While whimpering, I managed to tell her.

"I feel it again, sis. I feel worthless."

I couldn't believe that I told her the whole truth. Why did I say that? I had allowed her to see my vulnerability. That was a no-no. I regretted it immediately. Feeling ashamed, I prayed that she wouldn't judge me. I had been hurt by so many women—surely, I couldn't trust her. Would she be kind to me? Maybe, just maybe, she was one of the good ones. Then, it happened. Instead of being judgmental, she encouraged me. I sat in shock.

She spoke words of faith, kindness, and peace to me. My heart softened and opened. My ears perked up, my back straightened, and my heart recognized the language she was speaking: love. She also prayed for me. I felt calm.

We walked back to the salon chair together. I made eye contact with another stylist. No words were spoken, but I felt like she was judging me. I couldn't care less, though. I felt encouraged.

As the stylist turned my chair in front of the mirror, I smiled widely. Now relieved, I noticed that my hair was full of feathered curls, and my spirit was lifted higher! I am so grateful that my stylist loved me through those difficult moments. Her intercessory prayer invited peace to enter my heart. I felt so much better within. The hairstyle was just an added bonus.

To this day, I still love getting beautified; however, the authentic peace that fuels me ain't found in no salon! I seek peace from the Lord; I find it in the Word and amongst His people. When I don't have the strength to find or seek it, He delivers it to me. Oh, what a mighty God I serve. Jesus is the truth!

Sharing Peace

Later that same day, I walked into the nail salon to get my scheduled manicure and pedicure. My appointment was at 6 p.m. The nail technician was very friendly, but I could tell that she was tired. She walked very slowly; she had clearly been working all day. I silently prayed for her strength. She kindly asked me if I wanted something to drink. As I sat down in the comfortable massage chair, I thanked her for bringing me water. Light, relaxing music played while I enjoyed a book. I overheard the manager talking to my technician.

"Do you want to work tomorrow? Paul just called out," the manager offered.

"Aw, man, I can't. Wish I could. Need the money. I don't have anyone to watch my children," my technician responded.

My heart felt for her. I looked deeply into her teary eyes and could see the tug of war taking place in her mind. I could see that she wanted to work; however, she needed a break and she loved her children. While she took care of my nails, I learned that she had two small children and had recently moved to Tallahassee. Our shared love of family deepened our connection.

Before she painted my nails, I stood up and asked my nail technician if I could hug her. She said "yes" with a huge smile, and there we stood. I extended the same grace I received earlier that day, and she accepted it.

I held her the way my stylist held me. I was shown love, and now it was my turn. I prayed that she, too, would experience peace. Before I left, I shared local childcare resources with her. I wanted her to have a good day, too.

"Thank you! Thank you," she said.

My day had come full-circle. I gave the gift that I had been given—love. What an honor.

And just like Jesus commanded the storm to be still, so can you and I. We can speak to our circumstances and command peace to come into our hearts. Sis, we can experience perfect peace, the ultimate calm.

Keeping the Peace

Have you ever had a knot in your hair? Knots do not discriminate; therefore, every woman can relate to this. How did the knot get into your hair in the first place? Knots always seem to form out of nowhere. Maybe you went swimming, used too much gel, or simply washed your hair. If your hair is really curly, you are bound to have a few knots because where curls are, knots tend to follow. Sis, how do you get your knots out? Keeping it real, if I have a weave, I am not so gentle with those knots. I have no problem cutting the hair out, since it isn't real—or, at least, it isn't my own. However, if I'm wearing my natural curls, I'm patient with them. I usually spray my hair with a detangling product first. Then, I handle my hair with care by combing through it to make sure all the knots are out.

If a friend and I had a disagreement and both of us felt that our friendship was worth saving, we both would have to agree to do everything we could to save it. If our disagreement was a knot, we would agree to comb it out together. Therefore, navigating through the misunderstanding would require maturity from both of us as we patiently and carefully comb it out. When a relationship is valuable, combing out the knot—the disagreement—is the only option. Plain and simple, if one of us felt that the friendship was dispensable, the friendship would be over. A strong relationship is valuable. Therefore, a strong balm of truth, strong conditioner of time, or dab of distance can help to mend the relationship, thus removing all of the tangles. Rob Base was absolutely correct when he wrote, "It takes two to make things go right." I challenge you to seek to untangle any type of worthy relationship instead of cutting it off.

Inner Peace

I always wanted to create something that would impact women's lives. I dreamed of writing books for years. Even though it took a long time, I'm glad I waited on the specific directions from the Lord. Because I was obedient, I wrote the book He created my fingers to write. Every word you are reading came to me from the Lord. I vividly remember sitting down in front of the computer early in the morning at our kitchen table, typing nonstop. Those downloads from Heaven are real.

When I left my full-time job, I picked up my pen and started journaling again. It was January of 2019 and I was inspired to start anew. All it took was a conversation for me to receive a referral to a phenomenal publisher. I smiled as I locked the details into my phone. I will call her next week, I thought to myself. Monday came and I didn't call. When Tuesday came, I took a deep breath and called her nervously. We connected instantly. Her energy was dynamic and the numbers fit my budget. It was about to be on! I signed the contract later that week. I called Louis and told him the news. "Baby, I'm about to write my book!"

A couple weeks passed. I had been writing down my thoughts, and by now, my notes were pretty much all over my office. Good gracious, there were so many. I finally sat down and asked the Lord to settle my spirit. This book was not going to come from a bunch of sticky notes I had written over the years. I knew this was my opportunity to share His vision of Beautiful Healing; I couldn't and wouldn't dare to do this alone. I sought the Lord often. I prayed for patience and resilience to complete my goal and be a finisher. This was going to take time and I would develop my skill meticulously.

As soon as I would sit down to write, I wanted to check my email, respond to text messages, and scroll down the Facebook timeline. In addition to the distractions, once I gained the motivation to begin, I had a hard time completing my tasks. Yup, I was a procrastinator. Sis, I knew that I wanted to write this book; I simply had no idea how to even start.

Some mornings, I felt discouraged. I questioned if I should even be writing a book. I wanted to give up. Mama wasn't a phone call away anymore. I didn't know what to do, so I did what I figured she would tell me to do—pray. I started praying before I wrote. I kept praying, even if I didn't hear anything from God. What did He want me to write? Soon after, the motivational thoughts began to flow. I started reading scriptures daily. I began to think good thoughts about my abilities, my life, and my legacy. Before long, the writing flowed like water gushing from a fire hydrant. I didn't have to force anything. I scheduled short breaks to stretch, listen to a song, and meditate on the word of God. Every day, I chose to dig deep, dig deep, dig deep. I wouldn't write a word without the Lord's guidance.

I promised myself that absolutely nothing would stand in the way of the completion of my manuscript. I decided to dust off the binder I received from the Adult Learning and Education Center. I reviewed the sections about distractibility, time management, and tips on prioritizing tasks. As I applied the tips, my executive functioning skills improved and I wrote fluidly for longer periods of time. Yay for progress!

While writing this book, I shed a lot of tears. There were days when I felt sorry for myself. I felt as though life was harder for me because I think differently. The truth was that I harbored shame for years because I felt unsuccessful in just about every part of my life. Sure, I was a beauty queen in college, but what could I really do? What was I good at? Aha! I had found it: writing was my joy. It was cathartic for me. I began to heal from the heartaches caused by disappointments. My crying days were over. This was living!

When I write, I feel as though every part of me is being reset to the purest version of myself. I enter a world where there is no time, no anxiety attacks, no fear, no depression. I find myself at the table of creativity and there is plenty of room for me; room to sit, contribute, share, and play; room to be myself without being misunderstood. In this world, I am who I was created to be: just another woman who is healing beautifully.

During the writing process, I realized that as long as I am alive, I will be healing from something, and that is okay. When the negative thoughts emerged, I still somehow managed to hold hope's hand. I dug my heels in even deeper. I knew with every fiber of my being that I could finish my book. After a while, confidence welled up within me. I kept praying and using my tools day after day. My heart was in the game now. I would finish! I would win this time.

I don't know what you have struggled with, sis, but what I do know is that you can make peace with it. You don't have to wrestle with it all your life. Healing is not linear. Due to the complexities of life, you may think you are 100 percent healed in one area, only to reach another season in your life and realize that you, in fact, have not yet fully healed. We all know we are only human. The difference between a healed person and an unhealed person is that a healed person responds to a wound, whereas an unhealed person reacts. That seemingly minuscule lifestyle change in itself reveals a healed approach! That alone is worth celebrating.

I'm a witness that a woman can dig her heels in and complete things that she never thought were possible. Sis, all you have to do is decide what really matters. Remember to stay present. Trips down memory lane are messy. Stay focused on the now. It is incredibly rewarding to be an overcomer! I am stronger for walking it out, rather than giving up, on my path of Beautiful Healing.

Plan for Peace

These days, I prioritize peace. Seriously, I intentionally plan my days with peace in mind. I start my day by praying, writing my intentions, and believing that peace is mine. I take my empty hands, put them together with my thumbs crossed, and close my eyes. Prayer changes things.

Prayer

Lord, Jesus, it's me, Felicia. Thank You for this day. I am so
glad to be Your child. I honor You, Lord. Please clear my path
on my way on this new day. Lord, grant me peace.
Give me the strength to remember who I am in You.
Give me the truth! Help me to courageously obey Your ways.
Lord, I receive the peace that You have created for me on
this Earth. I love You.

Amen.

NOTE TO
SELF

1. *How do you define peace?*

_____

_____

_____

_____

_____

_____

_____

_____

_____

_____

_____

_____

_____

_____

2. _If peace was a tangible object, what would it be?_

Does it have a smell? Texture? Shape? What feeling would it offer?

_____

_____

_____

_____

_____

_____

_____

_____

_____

_____

_____

3. _Where do you find peace?_

_____

_____

_____

_____

_____

_____

_____

_____

_____

_____

_____

_____

_____

_____

4. Once you have found peace, what steps do you take to

sustain it?

_____

_____

_____

_____

_____

_____

_____

_____

_____

_____

_____

_____

NOTE TO
SELF

5. What are your takeaways from this letter?

Love Letter 6
Worth

Why Do Women Question Their Worth?

I've learned that women question their worth because they've been conditioned to do so by society. We are taught that we should not make waves and rock the boat, but instead compassionately tend to others. We are taught that we always need to be aware of how we impact others. Many women have been taught that in certain ways, we are a problem. For example, many of us have heard at least one of the following:

- Don't wear that tight outfit.
- Stop being so aggressive.
- Stop acting like you think you are all that!
- Don't wear that tight outfit!
- Stop dressing like a slob! Wear nicer clothes that compliment your figure!
- Why are you so loud?
- Speak up!
- Why are you so quiet all the time?!
- Stop being so aggressive!
- You should bolder!
- Stop acting dumb!
- You're too fat!
- You're too skinny!
- Why don't you have a job? You must be lazy.
- Why don't you stay home with your kids? You must not love them.
- Why are you still single? Your standards must be too high.
- Why did you get married so young? You must have settled for the first man to ask.
- Why don't you have any kids?
- Why does she have so many kids?
- Her skin is too dark.
- Her skin is too pale.
- You wear too much makeup!
- You don't wear enough makeup!
- Your hair is too thin. Add extensions, sis.
- Your hair is too thick. Tell your stylist to thin it out for you.

Dear Sister,

Worthiness is likened to an internal dialogue that we have with ourselves. The words in that dialogue reveal the level of worthiness or unworthiness that resides in our hearts. We're constantly asking ourselves if we are good enough or talented enough. The self-esteem, confidence, and self-reliance—or lack thereof—all tell the true story of how we view ourselves and, thus, how worthy we are in our own eyes.

Worth's Value

Knowing your worth establishes a valuable standard. The way a woman feels about herself affects every choice she makes. A woman who realizes her worth simply navigates life differently. I once relied on the world to tell me who I was and what I was worth. The world changes so fast, so I never really knew who I was or if I was worthy enough. Sis, it was exhausting! When I turned to God's word regarding my worth, I found the truth. Does your worth come from the world or the word of God? Let's examine further.

Worth from the World

Once upon a time, I sought my worth from the world. I searched for validation from friends, strangers, and social media. I hid in plain sight, conforming to whatever environment I was present in at that time. I wanted to fit in with others, and since each person is different, I had to be ready to shift my demeanor and mannerisms at any given moment. Since I lacked self-confidence, I relied on the opinions of others regarding my decisions about my appearance, worldview, and career.

I silenced my uniqueness and questioned myself. I long for you to acknowledge that you are one-of-a-kind; built to stand, not to hide. The Lord desires for His daughters to know specifically how worthy and loved they are and to live peaceful, unapologetic lives. Quite frankly, wearing masks wears a woman out. I am grateful that we can rest in the Lord's will for our lives according to Psalm 62:1, "I am at rest in God alone; my salvation comes from Him."

Sound familiar, sis? This conditioning has been imposed on us women since we were very young girls. We were taught to second-guess ourselves.

Worth from the Word

Oh, yes, You shaped me first inside, then out; You formed me in my mother's womb. I thank You, High God—You're breathtaking! Body and soul, I am marvelously made! — Psalm 139: 13-14. Finding my worth in the Word looks like this:

- I acknowledge that I was created in God's image (Genesis 1:27).
- I refer to scripture when I feel like I am not good enough.
- I realize that my worth is not dependent upon how much I accomplish.
- I read Proverbs 31 often.
- I no longer strive for perfection.
- I clearly comprehend that my life has great purpose.
- I realize that I am a flawed individual serving a flawless Lord.
- I consistently rely on the word of God for my decisions.
- I'm mindful of how my witness affects others.

Please don't misunderstand. I'm not always feeling the list above. Sometimes, I compare myself to other people. That never ends well. However, when I read 1 Peter 5:6, I'm quickly reminded of this truth: "Humble yourselves, therefore, under God's mighty hand, that He may lift you up in due time." I then ask the Lord to grant me the strength to trust His Word. The word of God does not change. I am well-aware that I am a child of God and I rest in that.

Stolen Worth

According to reported cases from the National Center for Victims of Crime, one in five girls has been molested. I remember being touched inappropriately by a non-family member. Shame used to sneak up on me, even though I did nothing wrong. I didn't tell anyone for many years. In college, I talked to a counselor about the situation for the first time ever. Interestingly, I felt instant relief in my stomach. I didn't realize how much stress I had been carrying with me for all those years. I am so glad I spoke to the counselor; in doing so, I learned about how much that incident affected my self-worth. I learned about trauma and that it was not uncommon to mourn over the peaceful innocence that was stolen from me. I never went back to see that counselor; however, that one visit was extremely helpful. Once innocence is stolen from someone, they are highly likely to experience shame that creates soul scars that may never fully heal. Unworthiness seeps into the heart of a girl and grows with her into womanhood. I felt unworthy, even though the perpetrator was 100 percent at fault. This experience is one of the reasons why I wrote this book.

So, maybe your story isn't that you were abused. Perhaps, you made a choice that haunts you. Or, maybe, you feel guilty for partaking in inappropriate behavior. It might be something entirely different for you. Sadly, millions of women are living with debilitating conditions that cause them to feel less than the best. The good news is that even if you've done awful things, grace is available to you. You are a worthy human being, deserving of respect and the highest kindness, regardless of what you have done or what has been done to you. You are not your bad choices. If you feel unworthy due to your past decisions and experiences, consider this question: Have you ever really imagined what a life of worthiness could feel like? Free yourself from judgment. Forgive yourself. You are worthy, sis!

Remember the third step to the path of Beautiful Healing? I committed to Christ with the understanding that God ultimately held the key that unlocked my true worth. The word of God says that I was made in the image of God; therefore, I have worth simply because God determined that I was worthy. He is the definer of true worth. Not only did He create me in His image; he also sent His beloved son, Jesus, to die in my place. John 3:16-18 (The Message Version) states, "This is how much God loved the world: He gave His Son, His one and only Son. And this is why: so that no one need be destroyed; by believing in Him, anyone can have a whole and lasting life. God didn't go to all the trouble of sending His Son merely to point an accusing finger and tell the world how bad it was. He came to help, to make the world right again. Anyone who trusts in Him is acquitted; any person who refuses to trust Him has long since been under the death sentence without knowing it, all because of their failure to believe in the one-of-a-kind Son of God when they are introduced to him."

When I learned this truth, I was freed from the world's standard of worthiness. Jesus is the only reason we have worth at all. Praise God!

This word also applies to you, sis. Read Romans 5:8. It says, "But God demonstrates His own love for us in this: While we were still sinners, Christ died for us." Amen!

Had it not been for the word of God, I would still wrestle with my worth. I don't know where I would be without the blueprint that the Lord has provided. The word of God is my standard. I had to understand that my worth is not based upon how I feel each day. I don't get to decide whether or not I am worthy on any given day. No outer force gets to tell me what I am worth.

If you are dealing with feelings of unworthiness, I have excellent news. Unworthiness can be served an eviction notice. My sister, regardless of whatever happened to you, you can be brand new. You are me and I am you. Healing is yours if YOU decide to embrace it and take the first step on your path. You can make the necessary shift in your life and decide to walk in the direction of Beautiful Healing. The thing is, sis, everything in this world is fleeting. It doesn't last. Just like sand in your hands, it slips away. I challenge you to look into your eyes in a mirror and acknowledge your innate worth. You are worthy! You are healing! You are free!

Confidence Personified

I was thinking about confidence the other day. I'm unsure why, but I used to believe that it only looks one way: bold and loud. In my eyes, if a woman was "confident," she wore red lipstick or uncomfortable, tall stilettos. Once upon a time, I worked at a super cute coffee shop. Located in a beautiful older building in downtown Valdosta, it was a pure beauty! It was there, in that coffee shop, where I witnessed just how quiet confidence could be.

One morning, a lady came in for her usual creme brulee latte. I noticed her carefree style first. Her cardigan was a pretty shade of baby pink. The line was very long, yet she waited patiently. She didn't just blend in with the other customers. This lady stood out.
In the afternoons, I usually waited on the few customers seated inside. One afternoon, that same lady approached me.

"Excuse me, what is your name? You look familiar," she said. I glanced up and then away quickly.

"My name is Felicia, ma'am." Shyness rained on my head. I didn't make much eye contact with her because she was beautiful! I didn't want to gaze at her. I felt an odd emotion—resistance mixed with fear. I was intimidated. "I'm not sure... where we have met... ma'am."

"Well, Felicia, you ought to smile more. Do you know that you are beautiful? Those big brown eyes were created to look up, young lady, not down," she said with a smile.

I couldn't help but look her into her eyes; she had my attention. I stood there in awe. I was perplexed. What just happened? Was she talking to me? When I returned to my dorm, I thought about what had happened at work. That encounter was a first. This marked the very first time a strikingly beautiful black woman, who was not a relative, was kind to me. I felt some sort of emotion I had never felt before. I felt seen.

That night, I told myself I was beautiful, and the next morning, I smiled when I glanced at my reflection in the mirror. I was empowered and I felt good inside. I soon learned that the incredible woman I had met was a brilliant Communications professor at Valdosta State University. I would eventually become one of her students. Not once did she announce that she knew she was beautiful, smart, and capable. She wasn't that kind of lady. Oh, but every time I was in her presence, I clearly could hear her quiet confidence. She knew she was extraordinary; in fact, she owned it without ever saying a word. I had a full-circle moment when I read her words in a letter of recommendation that she drafted on my behalf for a job opportunity. It read, "It is with great humility that I recommend Felicia Williams for this role. She always tells me that I am her role model; however, what she doesn't know is that she inspires me to be the best me that I can be. I have never met anyone like Felicia, and I've got a feeling I never will." All I could do was smile.

So, sis, what does confidence look like to you?

A Woman's Worth

Sis, remember that you are not defined by anything that has happened to you. You have to believe that for yourself, though. Dig deep in the word of God and discover how worthy you are. Remember that you cannot "work hard enough" to feel true worth.

Yep, I said it. You are worthy because Jesus died for you. Find your worth in the Word, sis. If you still experience feelings of unworthiness while pursuing a deeper understanding of God's word, don't be afraid to find out why. It's not good to live like this; I want better for you.

Wisdom has taught me that reflection is a good thing. Don't be afraid to pursue healing. Be where your feet are. Settle down. Time is moving fast enough. Savor the stillness, sis. Life is worth it. Start by putting the phone down. Instead, prop your feet up. Lay down your distractions, sis. Again, life is worth it. Live in peace and rest in peace.

Social Media and Worth

I limit time on all social media platforms for a reason. Social media is great for marketing purposes. Emotional health? Not so much. Social media can easily become a trap if used incorrectly. Social media—for example, Instagram, the platform known for vivid visuals—can cause a lot of traffic within the mind. Social media taps into one's insecurities. What starts out as admiration can take a turn quickly. I define envy as admiration gone just a little bit too far. I am not exempt, sis. I have learned my triggers. When I find myself being captivated by Instagram posts, I rein myself in. I remember when I used to look deeply into the lives of people I admired. Feelings of jealousy would rise up. Everything just looked so perfect! Any moment I spent comparing myself to others was a moment wrongly invested. I prayed to the Lord to help me break this unhealthy habit. I didn't want to experience these feelings.

Nowadays, I have only positive thoughts when I see a woman winning on the 'gram. I call her blessed. If I find that I'm stumbling and social media is just too much to handle, I log off. If you find yourself stumbling, sis, take a deeper look at what you are dwelling on. What are you giving your energy to? Reflect. Challenge those thoughts. Ask yourself, "Is this healthy?" Then, take the necessary action to pivot forward. If you find yourself stumbling, it's alright to get off social media.

Goodnight, Worthy

I started posting nightly self-worth quotes on social media

because I was having a tough time in the evenings. I typically reflect on my days in the evenings, and somehow, I eventually started thinking about the things that didn't go well during my days. Sadly, I developed a silent habit of playing the negative game of comparison on social media. Even though I had Lou right by my side, I still self-harmed my spirit by comparing myself to others. I knew that envy is admiration gone too far. I knew that this was a dead-end habit and I would eventually have to come to terms with it.

One night, I decided to step into new behavior. Why not focus on what really mattered from my day, like the excellent choices I made? I decided to write posts to encourage myself. I wanted to stop feeling awful about my days. That night, I wrote my first #goodnightworthy post. I didn't have a grand brand that I was promoting; I simply wanted to be intentional. Now that I have shifted my focus, I go to bed every night knowing I'm worthy. I believe it now. Even if the day didn't go so well, I get to end my evening in a positive disposition because I choose to. If you don't like something, exchange it for something that you do like.

When I began to find my worth in the Word, I realized that I am made in the image of the Lord. In order to walk out His truth, I had to believe it for myself. The word of God never changes—you can count on that. The world's view changes by the second. I choose to stand on the firm foundation of the word of God. How about you? Even though the Word identifies that you are made in the image of the Lord, you may still stumble in this area. I say you should keep trusting the word of God until every inch of your heart believes it.

You are worthy,
Felicia

Prayer

Dear Lord,
I know these memories of pain are not mine to carry.
I'm giving all my heartache, fears, and struggles to You.
Your word says that You love me and I want to believe
that. I really do. Please help me.

Amen.

1. On a scale of 1-10 (1 being the lowest and 10 being the highest), how would you rate your self-worth?

_____

_____

_____

_____

_____

_____

_____

_____

_____

_____

_____

NOTE TO
SELF

2. *How do you define worth?*

_____

_____

_____

_____

_____

_____

_____

_____

_____

_____

_____

_____

NOTE TO
SELF

3. Can you pinpoint seasons in your life when you doubted your worth? What factors led you to doubt your worth?

_____

_____

_____

_____

_____

_____

_____

_____

_____

_____

_____

_____

SELF

4. How is unworthiness showing up in your life currently?

What can you do to change this?

_____

_____

_____

_____

_____

_____

_____

_____

_____

_____

_____

_____

_____

NOTE TO
SELF

5. What realistic actions can you take this week to build your

self-worth? How can you maintain it?

_____

_____

_____

_____

_____

_____

_____

_____

_____

_____

_____

_____

Love Letter 7

Embracing Your Path

Hi, Sis!

While driving one day, it occurred to me that no matter how hard people try, they will never completely heal during their lifetimes. We all are in a continual state of healing while here on Earth. When we improve in one area of life, we are still deficient in another. I believe that the woman who realizes that healing is continual is more likely to naturally forge ahead in life, for she understands that setbacks will come. She is the woman who keeps going after climbing the challenging mountains of sacrifice and trudging through the valley of pain—I refer to this woman as a Warrior in Healing. She is an overcomer and knows what real transformation looks like. She possesses an unquenchable fire within her; she is truly a Warrior in Healing. This fire encourages her to live on, despite life's shortcomings. Warriors realize the power of the light within them. They use their light to see through the darkness in this broken world. They realize that they have God's imprint planted within them, and they won't give up until they find it! A Warrior in Healing realizes the value of the gift the Lord blessed her with and realizes that only she can share this gift with this world in a special way. She patiently digs, then digs deeper, all while trusting that the Lord will tell her all the details she needs. She rises early, exhibits purpose, and presses in. Warriors in Healing recognize that transformation takes place throughout life and not overnight.

I Have Learned

Sisters, the word of God is bigger than your storm. The Word has more power than your feelings. I have always found hope in His word. He has created us anew in Christ Jesus so that we can do good things. He planned for us long ago. He didn't ask me if I was a masterpiece. The Word is clear—"for we, that's all of His children, are God's masterpiece"—and that is what helps me with worthiness, beauty, and gifts. It's not up to me to decide if I'm worthy, gifted, or a masterpiece. My Creator already told me that I am all of these things, and then He put a gift inside of me: the gift to create. Guess what? I believe that children carry their Father's ways. Therefore, our Heavenly Father deposited characteristics within us to create because we are His and He is the Master Creator. I know that to find fulfillment and real joy is to operate in your gift and to do that which only you were created to do. That is the cure to jealousy, envy, and, well, any other divisive characteristic that threatens another beautiful sister created in the image of Christ. When the Lord revealed Beautiful Healing™ to me, I couldn't care less about what type of purse another woman owned or where she got her hair done. My heart swelled with goodness. Joy! Fulfillment! Holiness and righteousness took root in my heart and I am a more grateful woman now. I'm genuinely happy and joyful and I wouldn't dare tear another sister down. My cup runneth over. Thank you, Jesus, for the breakthrough! My sister, these are the things I have learned about believing and walking through the instructions of the word of God.

Sis, I am proud of you. You possess God-given gifts and the world needs to experience them. Are you ready to step onto your path of Beautiful Healing? I believe in you. I pray that all seven of these letters have encouraged you and will continue to encourage you as needed. Allow the words to mentor you on your path. If you get stuck, don't hesitate to reach out by emailing me at Felicia@BeautifulHealing.Life. I'm here to hold your hand through every step you take, sis! Now, I leave you with the official Beautiful Healing Mantra. The Lord gave me these words early one morning. Speak them boldly and with confidence! You can do life, sis! I believe in you.

Beautiful Healing Mantra

Restoration, I am coming for you! But first, I'm pushing the release button. I am now choosing to open the door to my heart and mind. I am equipped for the path ahead. I realize that healing occurs over a lifetime and not overnight. I want to know more about You, Lord. I will listen to learn. If I feel something hurting in my heart, I will not run away from it. I reject shame. As I travel, I will seek the truth, unlearn lies, and give myself grace.

Again, I will not run. This path is long and I will take my time to walk it out so that I don't miss You, Lord. If I see broken pieces, I will not get angry with myself; instead, I will use my hands to pray. By continuing on my path, I am illustrating just how worthy I am. I find my worth in the Word rather than in the world. I will not give up on this. I will be patient on my path.

If I get stuck, I will sound the alarm by praying and asking the Lord to help me. I don't have to go at this alone, for He is with me. I am safe. Even if I don't feel like it, I will continue. When I experience fear, I will not fold. I realize that there are no stupid questions—only unasked ones. I will not punish myself if I don't know the answers. It is okay to lack knowledge. As my heart opens, tears may fall down my face. I understand that tears are not a sign of weakness. It is healthy to release the heaviness I have felt but didn't realize I was carrying.

I believe that I can beautifully heal. I have decided that I am willing to discover answers and face myself. I stepped into greater the minute I purchased this book. Yes! I proclaim that I am not okay with staying the same. I was created for this. I am open to experiencing my Beautiful Healing. I'm willing. I'm looking ahead. I can look up and smile. I am listening. I accept myself just as I am. I am real. I am strong. I will embrace my path.

Today, I am taking my first step onto my path of Beautiful Healing.

NOTE TO
SELF

1. *What do you need to acknowledge?*

_____

_____

_____

_____

_____

_____

_____

_____

_____

_____

_____

_____

_____

2. How can reflection play a role in your potential progress?

_____

_____

_____

_____

_____

_____

_____

_____

_____

_____

_____

NOTE TO SELF

<u>3.</u> <u>In what ways has committing to Christ impacted your life?</u>

_____

_____

_____

_____

_____

_____

_____

_____

_____

_____

_____

_____

NOTE TO
SELF

4. _What obstacles are keeping you from stepping forward?_

5. _What are your takeaways from this book?_

_____

_____

_____

_____

_____

_____

_____

_____

_____

_____

_____

_____

_____

NOTE TO
SELF

6. <u>Write a love letter to yourself about your path of Beautiful</u>

<u>Healing.</u>

Felicia doesn't just preach about the pathway of Beautiful Healing—she's lived it. Her guidance and leadership was reaped by her own trials and tribulations. I've personally witnessed her infusion of purpose into her own journey to becoming a Healer of the human spirit. I look forward to seeing so many lives touched by what I already know: Felicia is a gift to the broken made new.

- Lee H. Williams II

I could write a book on how kind-hearted, honest, driven, and motherly Felicia Dilbert is. I lost my mom when I was 11 years old and Felicia's presence has given me the feeling I once felt—that someone cares for me unconditionally.

- Jordan DeBenedictis

Felicia is an awesome wife, friend, and sister. She's a Queen.

- Crystal Williams

Felicia is my sister, but she is like a second mom to me. Growing up, I admired her maturity and carefreeness. Now, I admire those same qualities, as well as her ability to channel creativity and newness. She is not only a motivator, but also an inspiration to us all.

- Lee Alisha Williams

Felicia is someone who truly cares about anyone she crosses paths with. Her sincerity shines through in every situation and she is someone who you can count on during the hard times in your life. She is always there with a ready ear and an open mind to provide judgement-free guidance and advice. She is truly a gift.   -
Stacy Hernandez

I met Felicia at church. I've had a glimpse of what a beautiful person she is. Through her writings, she has turned life's hardships into ministry. She speaks from her experiences and faith, and her writings have inspired me. I have been blessed by her friendship!

- Autumn Johnson

Felicia Dilbert is one in a million! I met her many years ago and the first thing I noticed about her was her smile! Her smile was as big, bright, and genuine as her heart. Felicia is a woman who consistently shows kindness. She's truly a free spirit—a breath of fresh air! She pours herself into anyone she serves. Felicia has a calm and playful demeanor that each of us should strive to possess. I have always admired her servant's heart, and for that, I am extremely thankful. Without words, she has pushed me to be a better me because of the way she lives her life and I will forever be grateful.

- Tyrika Morgan

Made in the USA
Columbia, SC
05 April 2021